HOW UNDERDOG WAS BORN...

HOW UNDERDOG WAS BORN...

by
Buck Biggers & Chet Stover

BearManor Media
2005

How Underdog Was Born
© 2005 by Buck Biggers and Chet Stover

for information, address:

BearManor Media
P. O. Box 750
Boalsburg, PA 16827

bearmanormedia.com

Cover design by Lloyd W. Meek
Pen and Inks by Chet Stover
Typesetting and layout by John Teehan

Published in the USA by BearManor Media

Library of Congress Cataloging-in-Publication Data

Biggers, Buck.
How Underdog was born / by Buck Biggers and Chet Stover.
p. cm.
Includes index.
ISBN 1-59393-025-9

I. Stover, Chet. II. Underdog (Television program) III. Title.

PN1992.77.U54B54 2005
791.45'72--dc22
2004027020

DEDICATION

For Victory Over Violence, Ince., a national non-profit organization dedicated to the creation of a positive force in the media. All authors' net profits derived directly from the sale of this book will be donated to Victory Over Violence, Inc.

Table of Contents

Introduction 1

How Underdog Was Born 5

Afterword 151

Storylines & Summaries 163

Index 191

Introduction

It was the night of March 6, 1995, at Harvard University in Cambridge. Tom Hanks, winner of the Best Actor Academy Award in 1994, and leading candidate for that honor in 1995, sat at a long banquet table in a room filled with members of the Boston press, as well as Harvard students. Although he was being very cooperative in answering questions about his past and present decisions, it was obvious to everyone that he was extremely weary.

And no wonder. Invited to Harvard to receive the Hasty Pudding Club's "Man of the Year" Award, Hanks' day had been busy. His morning had been devoted to criss-crossing the Harvard campus answering questions from students, professors and alumni. Lunch might have provided a brief respite. Instead, it had turned into a tiring seminar at Boston's popular Biba restaurant. And that evening, Hanks had donned pink spiked heels, a spangled bra, and a woman's auburn wig before going on stage at the Hasty Pudding Club, reminding the audience of his 1980 television series, *Bosom Buddies*. After tossing his pumps and bra to the audience, Hanks energetically tossed darts at pictures of those actors who would compete with him in three weeks at the Academy Awards. Finally, he had recreated his very athletic piano dance from the popular movie *Big*.

Now, as he faced the press, his lack of energy was apparent. But suddenly, a single, simple question completely changed the actor's countenance. As if by magic, his tiredness fell away, a broad smile brightened his face, and he was clearly excited. The question: "Do you remember a cartoon character named 'Underdog'?"

Hanks responded immediately. "Underdog? Of course I do." And he recited, "When Polly's in trouble/ I am not slow/ It's hip, hip, hip/ And *away* I go." And now he burst into song, waving his arms as if leading an orchestra:

"When in this world
The headlines read
Of those whose hearts
Are filled with greed,
Who rob and steal
From those in need.
Then to this spot
With blinding speed
Goes Underdog . . .
Underdog . . ."

Pausing, he yelled to the audience: "Sing it, everybody!"

Everyone joined in as the actor continued to sing, right on key, even without accompaniment to guide him:

"Speed of lightning,
Roar of thunder,
Fighting all who
Rob or plunder
Underdog . . .
Underdog."

The question to Hanks about Underdog had come from Nancy Purbeck, founder and president of the nonprofit organization Victory Over Violence, Inc., dedicated to "creating a positive force in the media and, thereby, reducing the cynicism and negativity which create a climate of violence." This organization had chosen Underdog as its mascot and media image.

Extremely pleased by the tremendous enthusiasm the mention of Underdog had evoked with Tom Hanks and his audience, Ms. Purbeck asked "Underdog" creators Buck Biggers and Chet Stover if they would star Underdog in a live musical which would be performed in Boston as a fund-raiser for Victory Over Violence, Inc.

More than two years later, at 8:30 P.M. on October 29, 1997, in the Oval Room of Boston's Copley Plaza Hotel, an overflow crowd was watching the live musical *Simon Says...Make Me King*, starring Underdog, Sweet Polly Purebred, Simon Barsinister and Cad Lackey. Among the luminaries in the audience, Boston's Mayor Thomas Menino sat at a down-front center table, leading the applause.

By way of print, radio, TV and outdoor billboards, grownup fans of Underdog had been encouraged to come and lend their hero their support in his attempt to prevent Simon Barsinister from filling the streets of Boston with violence.

In the course of the play, Simon sang, "Negative People are the People Meant for Me," Underdog sang, "Anything's Possible if You Believe in You," and Sweet Polly Purebred sang, "Positive People are the People Meant for Me."

When the performance concluded, the applause was thunderous, complete with bravos, cheers and whistles. And as Mayor Menino left the room he was overheard singing, "Positive People are the People Meant for Me."

At the after-play party, amid champagne and hors d'oeuvres, the possibility of an "Underdog" book was mentioned, and person after person expressed their enthusiasm for the project as they spoke of how much the series had affected their lives.

There were many questions this group wanted answered in the book, such as how and why the series came to be created, what led the creators to villains like Simon Barsinister and Riff Raff, why Underdog spoke in rhyme, where he got his powers—"Is he from another planet, like Superman?"—but the question which did more than any other to motivate Buck and Chet to write this book came from a 34-year-old television reporter. What she wanted to know was, "Did you know when you were doing it…when you were creating 'Underdog'…that the series would be so different…so popular and everything? So special?"

One

Did Buck and Chet have any inkling at the beginning that Underdog would turn out to be so special? No doubt about it. Even before they had decided on the character or concept, even before they began work on the project, things happened that had *never* happened before—like the fact that the new assignment from Gordon Johnson was going to be a contest, a competition. Buck and Chet had never had that before; never had to compete head-to-head with another creative team.

Even Buck's plane trip to the meeting with Gordon was different. Buck had made this trip at least 25 times, working on other series he and Chet had created, and not once had anything unusual happened. Not once had the plane or the pilot or the stewardess or any of the passengers ever done a single thing to make one flight stand out from another. Not until Buck flew to New York for the June 1963 meeting with Gordon Johnson, the meeting which would lead to the birth of Underdog.

What happened on this flight was that a performer came aboard. A celebrity. This was a major difference already. Buck had never seen a celebrity of any kind on this dinky airline until now. And no wonder. The planes were those ancient-looking DC-3s with the tiny tail wheel which forced you to walk downhill getting on and uphill getting off. You wouldn't expect to find a big name here. But that's what happened this trip. And the difference didn't stop there. It wasn't just that there was a celebrity on board. It was what the celebrity did on the plane. His actions. They would play a definite role in the birth of Underdog.

When this guy came on board, Buck was already seated, about a half-way back on the right side of the cabin. The celebrity was tall and a bit

5

heavy-set with dark hair, a ruddy complexion and a full moustache. He came up the red-carpeted aisle wearing a brown suit and a hat and tie and carrying some kind of periodical under his right arm.

This was not just any celebrity. This was Ray Goulding, one of Buck's favorite performers. He was half of the highly offbeat, highly popular comedy team "Bob and Ray." They'd had a radio show for many years, performed in clubs, had a TV series, and they had provided the voice for a much talked about series of animated TV commercials for a popular beer. They'd even done a series of radio commercials for General Mills, written and directed by Chet. In person or on TV, radio or records they did comedy routines that were usually interviews, mostly Bob playing some sort of announcer interviewing Ray, who would be anything from a cranberry grower who had never heard of cranberry sauce, to a man who took forever to complete a sentence because he was the champion Slow Talker of America.

Goulding passed by Buck and took a seat maybe three rows back on the other side of the aisle. The plane was less than a third full, but the comic proved to be the last passenger boarding (the airline had probably planned it that way, royal treatment for their first celebrity). The outside steps disappeared, the door was closed, and the plane began to taxi out onto the runway.

It only took a few minutes to get in the air and start climbing, but that was enough for Buck to turn his head to one side, close his eyes and begin drifting toward sleep. He was too tired to work, having been up late at a party the night before. Unless he could make up for the lost sleep, he would feel the time on this flight had been wasted. So he was ready to drift off quick as a wink. But the moment the plane leveled out something happened that made sleep highly unlikely.

It was only a small sound at first. You might call it a snicker. Buck heard it and found himself irritably wondering what the hell it was and why. But he continued to try to sleep...until the next sound. This was no snicker. It was an out-and-out cackle. And it kept going.

Buck sat up and turned around, looked to the other side of the airplane at Ray Goulding and, sure enough, the comic was the culprit. His hands were wide apart as he held open a newspaper or large magazine just below his face. He was reading and turning the pages slowly, and already his cheeks were growing pink with laughter.

Sleep? Forget it. Normally that would have irritated Buck like a dripping water faucet, but not this time. First of all, he liked and admired Ray

Comic Ray Goulding of "Bob and Ray," hidden behind a newspaper and laughing hilariously on the plane from Hyannis to LaGuardia.

Goulding's work. And, second, how the hell could you stay irritated at anyone who was laughing in a way that made you feel happy?

The laughter came in bursts. Clearly, Goulding was responding to what he was reading, his eyes scanning the type for a minute, then another cackle, more silent scanning, then more cackling. This man seemed to be having the time of his life, thanks to what he was reading. And it lasted all the way from Hyannis to New York, except for a very brief period when Dinky Airlines served coffee in McDonald's-quality paper cups. Nothing but the best.

By the time they reached LaGuardia, Buck was dying to know the name of the publication Goulding had been reading, but he figured he'd never get a chance to learn. It was probably some kind of special comedy publication, he supposed; maybe a trade paper used by comics to build routines. And Goulding would never leave it behind.

Buck was wrong. As he kept his seat and let Goulding pass by, he noticed that the comedian carried nothing with him. Why? Going back to the seat, Buck grabbed up the periodical, some kind of newspaper, stuffed it into his briefcase like a thief, and hurried down the aisle. He would look at the paper on his way into Manhattan.

But first, he had to get a taxi.

LaGuardia had a lousy system that made finding an empty cab about as easy as finding a flea on a black dog at midnight. What they did was, the minute you stepped off a plane, their signs started directing you to the lower level for a taxi. Sign after sign after sign. And when you got there, they funneled you like cattle into a narrow fenced-in corridor on the sidewalk and that led you, one cow at a time, to a line of cabs as endless as the highway to hell. The wait was long and uncomfortable, and especially unappealing to Buck today because he was anxious to peruse that paper Ray Goulding had left behind.

So, instead of obeying the airport signs, Buck went up to the upper level where taxis dropped off passengers. Drivers were not supposed to pick up anyone there, but they dreaded getting into that long line of cabs on the lower level. So, if you arrived just as they were dropping off a passenger, they were more than happy to hustle you into their taxi.

That was what Buck did now, immediately getting a cab. As soon as the driver had his instructions and they were on their way to Manhattan, Buck popped open his briefcase eager to get a look at Goulding's paper.

The minute it was out, Buck was shocked. This was no trade paper, no publication to help comics develop routines. This was nothing but an ordinary newspaper. This was the *Boston Globe*! Laughter on every page? How could that be?

The taxi sped across the Triboro Bridge, past the single homes and the duplexes, and two-story, three-story, four-story tenements, all mostly gray, the original white darkened by the city's soot. And while the buildings whizzed by, Buck examined the *Globe*:

WALLACE BLOCKS DOORWAY TO INTEGRATION, read a front page headline. Was that laugh-provoking? The picture with the headline looked extremely serious—Governor Wallace in a pin-striped suit attempting to prevent the enrollment of a black student in an Alabama college. What was so funny about this redneck governor taking his stand in favor of second-class citizenship for Negroes?

DIEM DENIES COUP ATTEMPT, read another headline, this one showing a picture of the South Vietnam president facing reporters as he denied the rumor. Was that humorous? How? Why?

Another story showed row after row of airliners on the ground and a headline which read, FLIGHTS GROUNDED BY AIRLINE STRIKE. Funny? Not even a smile.

And so it went, page after page of headlines, some with pictures, none with humor—stories which became no more comical when thoroughly explored. They were simply not funny bits. None of them. Not one. As Manhattan drew nearer, Buck asked himself how this could be. How could Ray Goulding have found so much laughter in such serious material?

Buck returned to the front page, trying to remember how Goulding had looked as he laughed; then thought of some typical "Bob and Ray" routines. And, suddenly, something weird happened. Looking at the George Wallace story, Buck saw it in a slightly different way: WALLACE BLOCKS DOORWAY TO INTEGRATION. Instead of the Governor in a pin-striped suit, portraying the dignified protector of the Old South, imagine him standing in the doorway wearing a white sheet with eye-holes, or maybe the sheet is stuffed into his back pocket, but hanging out. Buck laughed. Funny. Just see it a little differently. Like a cartoon. That brought humor.

What about the DIEM DENIES COUP ATTEMPT? Instead of having Diem look perfectly normal as he faces the TV cameras, imagine him naked, a sheet of paper covering his vitals, in an office which has obviously been ransacked and shot to pieces. Funny, but too far. Not naked. Make him only half-naked, half his uniform shot away, the half the TV cameras don't see. Same with his office. Just a facade. And he's denying anything happened. Good. Funny.

What about FLIGHTS GROUNDED BY AIRLINE STRIKE?…Don't just read the headline. Visualize it. A union man with a big sign. A huge sign. The union man holds up the sign with one hand and it reaches way up to the sky, so high and so big that planes are crashing into it and falling to the ground. FLIGHTS GROUNDED BY AIRLINE STRIKE. There was humor there—a little black, maybe, but funny.

It was the same with the other headlines. The formula worked. Take a real subject, a serious subject, and move it slightly to the left or right. See it just a wee bit off-center, and it turned into laughter—related to satire and parody and farce and camp, but not quite any of these; not as far as they would go. The laughter came only if the words or story or picture were *almost* true, almost reality.

Buck thought about leaving the newspaper behind. But then he shook his head and stuffed the paper into his briefcase. Somehow he knew it was important. He ought to discuss it with Chet.

Two

The Gamecock was a mid-price restaurant at the corner of Madison Avenue and 43rd Street. The food and drink were adequate but certainly not spectacular, and neither was the décor or atmosphere. But the restaurant was very convenient—only two blocks from Dancer-Fitzgerald-Sample, the advertising agency where Gordon Johnson was one of the top executives—and even more important it had one table that Gordon called "my meeting room" because of its privacy. Actually this was simply a table and two banquettes in an alcove set in the restaurant's rear wall, the only such area in the restaurant. It served well as a place to conduct business in confidence.

When Buck arrived, Gordon was already in his "meeting room" sipping a vodka martini on the rocks. He reached over to shake hands. "I see you're still wearing that goddamn beard," he said with a smile.

They were a contrast in size and appearance. At six feet two, Gordon towered over Buck, and in conformance with advertising executives in those days, Gordon was clean shaven, wore black shoes, a white shirt, striped tie, and a conservative suit—blue serge today. But Buck, who had worked for Gordon three years before, had changed considerably since giving up advertising for TV shows.

His suit had been traded in for slacks and a colorful sports jacket. His tie was gone and the black shoes had become brown loafers. But the biggest change was a small, neatly trimmed goatee.

As Buck slid into the banquette opposite him, Gordon asked, "What happened to the moustache?"

Buck smiled and shook his head. "Gordy, I never had a moustache.

11

The Gamecock "meeting room" where Gordon gave Buck the challenge that led to "Underdog."

Never." Gordon asked the same question almost every time they got together.

"Oh. But you're still wearing the beard. You sure as hell don't' look like an advertising guy anymore."

"I didn't plan to keep it, Gordon. A lot of us grew them on the Cape to celebrate the 300th anniversary of the founding of Chatham. But when I shaved it off, my daughter hated the way I looked, said I looked like a chipmunk."

Gordon laughed. "How old is Vicki now?"

"Six."

"You're going to be in deep shit if you start letting women run your life when they're only six years old. You ought to at least wait until she's a teenager."

The waiter came, and Buck ordered the same drink Gordon was having. The waiter asked, "Do you want some menus now?"

"No, no," Gordon answered quickly. "We'll be working before we eat. Just keep the glasses full."

When they were alone, Gordon said, "What did you guys think of Cy's ideas for *Tennessee?*"

Buck shrugged. "They're okay. They duplicate a lot of what we already had, so we can use some of them—at least the educational part. He doesn't understand the rest."

They were talking about Buck and Chet's second cartoon series, *Tennessee Tuxedo and His Tales*, due to debut on Saturday morning in three months. Cy Plattes, a General Mills executive involved in the purchase of such series, had submitted some ideas for future episodes of *Tennessee*.

"Good," said Gordon. "The fact that he's sending in ideas for all these new episodes pretty much guarantees a second order...*if* we get top ratings when the series debuts."

Buck winked. "We will. *Tennessee* is terrific." His martini came then. They raised their glasses in a toast, took a swallow of the drinks, and returned to the discussion of opportunities (and problems) with the *Tennessee* series. It was this Buck had assumed that was the purpose of their meeting, and, to some degree, that was true. They spent some time discussing problems they'd been having and what needed to be done between this meeting and the debut of *Tennessee* in September.

But by the time they were lifting their second drinks, a different subject was about to begin. "Have you guys got anything new?" Gordon asked, as if the question had no special importance.

"We're always noodling," said Buck, "but until we get the last of the *Tennessee* order ready, we won't be spending a lot of time on new stuff."

Gordon grinned. "Maybe you'll have to." He let it hang there.

Something was up, Buck knew immediately. Gordon had news, and he was purposely taking his time about delivering it, enjoying the situation. "What do you mean?" Buck asked. "Why should we have to start on something new?"

"Because things are different with the networks now. You've been away a few years, you know. It's not the same."

"What?"

"They moved up the timetable. Right after the new shows debut on Saturday morning, the networks will be ready to talk about next year. So if General Mills wants more time periods—in the *best* Saturday time—they have to be ready with new series. Ready to talk turkey."

"How soon after the new shows debut?"

"The middle of October."

When he said nothing more, Buck asked, "Are you saying that General Mills is already set on programming additional time-slots next season?" (At this time, and until the 1970s, many corporations like General Mills typically purchased TV series from production companies, after obtaining network approval on the pilot episode. They placed them in a particular time-slot on the network, guaranteeing the network that the corporation would buy all or most of the commercials in that series. Later, the networks would stop this practice so that they could exercise stricter control over program content and quality. But in the 50s and 60s, General Mills and other large corporations supplied a major portion of network programming, especially for children.)

Now, Gordon nodded. "The Mills has to have more commercial time. New cereals alone would make that a must. And Cheerios' increased sales puts the need way over the top. We've got to have more time."

Buck was getting excited. "So, General Mills wants a new series already. That's great." He and Chet had not expected the Mills to be in the market for another property until well into 1964.

Still grinning like a Cheshire cat, Gordon said, "Not just one. Maybe two."

"Two?" Surprise was turning into shock. "Two new half-hour series for Saturday morning?"

Gordon was enjoying himself. "That's right, two. One on NBC and one on ABC."

"That's great."

"They'll put the series they like best on NBC."

Sure, Buck could understand that. ABC was relatively new. Not even a full Saturday morning schedule. An NBC time-slot would offer considerably more potential viewers than on ABC. "Are you saying you want us to come up with two new concepts?"

Gordon shook his head. "Just one. You guys come up with one and Ward and Scott will come up with one." Ward and Scott were the creators of *Rocky and Bullwinkle* which General Mills had bought and put on ABC. "If the Mills likes both series," Gordon went on, "they'll put their first choice on NBC, and the other one on ABC."

"So it's…it's going to be a kind of contest. Is that what you mean?" They had never been given such an assignment before.

"That's the idea. You'll both get a shot. Hopefully you'll both sell a series."

"And the best one gets to NBC."

"Right." Gordon winked. "And all this is strictly confidential, Buck— our talks with the networks, the fact that the Mills has an option on two time-slots, the competition with Ward and Scott—all of it. Keep it on a need-to-know basis."

Buck nodded. "Will do." He took a swallow of his martini. "Are there any guidelines for the series—like the educational assignment with *Tennessee?*"

"It's wide open. All I can tell you is that you've got to have a super series—and I mean *super*—if you want to get on NBC with this new show."

"But the kind of character and stories, that's wide-open for us?"

"Except for one thing," said Gordon, lowering his voice and smiling mysteriously. "Stay away from frogs."

Three

Did things really happen which pointed toward the new series being something special? They certainly did. Buck and Chet couldn't see it at the time, but there's no doubt these things happened. Remember Rod Serling's words? "Up ahead…The Twilight Zone." Well, maybe this wasn't exactly The Twilight Zone, but there were definitely signposts along the way. Consider the fact that Chet just happened to see one certain TV show at the time he and Buck were getting the Underdog assignment.

For a lot of people, seeing something on TV, whatever it is, might not be unusual. But what you have to understand is that Chet Stover seldom watched television. Even when he was a top creative guy with the advertising agency Dancer-Fitzgerald-Sample and was responsible for creating millions and millions of dollars worth of TV commercials, he watched little. In fact, early in his career when he first started creating TV commercials, he didn't even own a TV set.

Strangely enough, he had many times been mistaken for someone on TV, was even at times asked for his autograph. Medium height, trim build, short sandy hair brushed forward, he bore a striking resemblance to Ray Walston, the actor who played the title role in the very popular series *My Favorite Martian*. When this mistaken identity had first occurred, Chet had actually been forced to watch the series (for the first time) in order to see who it was he looked like!

And if he *almost* never watched nighttime TV, let it be known here that he *never*—never, never—watched daytime TV, considering it an utter waste of time (except, of course, for an occasional peek on Saturday morning to see his own handiwork). And, yet, it may well be that Underdog would never have been born if Chet Stover had not watched daytime television just six days before he met Buck to discuss the new order from the Mills. And Chet would never have watched daytime television if his younger son had not happened to be home sick with a cold.

It happened like this: When Buck had moved from New York to Cape Cod (once they had their cartoon business up and running), Chet had moved his family to a 60-acre farm in the hills of northwest Connecticut. While it wasn't exactly a working farm, it did have a large barn, outbuildings and a sprawling colonial farmhouse, part of which dated back to 1750. Chet's office-studio on the second floor was a large bright room and, opposite his desk, French doors opened to a small balcony and a marvelous view over the surrounding fields and distant hills.

This particular morning, the work was going well (sometimes it was like pulling teeth) and at about ten o'clock, Chet decided to take a break and went down the back stairs to the kitchen. While he was pouring his coffee, he heard talking and laughing coming from the TV room just off the kitchen and wandered over to see just what was so funny. He found his younger son, Evan, inside rather than outside because of a bad cold, lying on the couch and laughing uproariously at a rerun of *I Love Lucy*.

Despite the fact that he avoided daytime TV like a plague, Chet loved sharing with his sons *and* he was a practiced procrastinator who would do almost anything to put off work. He motioned to Evan to scoot over and sat down with his coffee to watch.

It was the classic Superman episode where Lucy is going all-out to give Little Ricky a blockbuster fifth birthday party. She has learned that George Reeves, the actor who played Superman, is in town and decides that he is the very person to make this event unforgettable. She immediately asks Big Ricky to use his show business connections to "invite" Superman to the birthday party. Then, without waiting to hear whether this is possible, goes right ahead and announces to one and all that the man of steel will come crashing in, thereby thrilling all the kids and outshining all the mothers. A coup!

Of course, Ricky is unable to enlist Superman and there is Lucy, stuck in a typical Lucy situation. What to do? Naturally, she decides to play Superman herself. At this point, Chet was hooked, not only because the show was genuinely funny, but also because he was lost in admiration for the ingenuity, inventiveness and skill of the writers—one craftsman appreciating the work of others. It added a whole new dimension to his television watching.

The TV room where Chet saw "I Love Lucy"

Lucy, enlisting the help of best friend Ethel, gets all rigged out in a ridiculous costume with a football helmet, baggy-saggy tights and a huge cape. Now they have to figure out how to make a dramatic entrance.

LUCY: Sometimes Superman will come crashing through the wall.

ETHEL: (*concerned*) But you know how Fred would feel about that.

LUCY: (*nodding*) Yeah, I'd better find some better way to have him come in.

What she hits on is to come in through the living room window. With the party in full swing, she crawls out on a narrow ledge high above the streets and awaits her big moment. Just then the "real" Superman *does* come crashing in, thanks to Big Ricky. The kids are ecstatic and so is Lucy. Unfortunately, she finds she can't get back inside to join the party. The window has slammed shut and there she stands on that narrow ledge. Pigeons drop on her; a rainstorm nearly drowns her. Misery. Finally in a hilarious scene, Superman rescues Lucy, then turns to Ricky and says, "You mean to say that you've been married to her for 15 years?...And they call *me* Superman!"

Chet sat there for a while thinking about what he had just seen and enjoyed immensely. He knew a class act when he saw one. And this had been a class act from start to finish. A minor comic masterpiece. He wondered if there was anything there they could use in a future *Tennessee* episode. *Tennessee* in sagging tights? Maybe. He filed it away in the back of his mind and went upstairs to work.

Weeks later, in a moment of desperate need, the memory of this episode would return.

Four

The 1812 House on Route 9 in Framingham, Massachusetts was a bed-and-breakfast inn which fairly oozed charm. Out front, the large black door of the gray clapboard building was framed by two white two-story columns with four black-trimmed windows on either side. The moment the door was opened, guests were greeted by the sound of taped violin music and the sight of dark wood everywhere—floors, walls, chairs, tables and a highly-polished bar where juice, coffee and Danish were served in the morning and alcoholic drinks at noon. Out back, the inn's rather limited number of rooms was supplemented by an inviting one-story motel.

The motel rooms doubled perfectly as work space, the inn's food and drink were excellent, the atmosphere was delightful, and the owner and his employees were always cordial and accommodating. But none of this had anything to do with the reason the inn had been chosen as the weekly meeting place for Buck and Chet. The choice had been made because, in terms of driving time, the 1812 House was almost equidistant from Buck's home on Cape Cod and Chet's home in Connecticut.

They had a long-standing arrangement with the 1812 House management to reserve one of the motel rooms every Wednesday and also a large round table in one corner of the inn's dining room where they would work through lunch.

The routine seldom varied.

Chet usually arrived first, roaring up from the Mass Pike in his tiny red and black TR-3 sports car which the cops often stopped just because it *looked* like it was speeding. Buck arrived a short time later in his small yellow beat-up Renault which often blew back and forth on Route 128 like a piece of paper. They went first for coffee and Danish, sitting at the bar and unwinding from the two-hour drive with small talk about families and other news until it was time to move onto the motel room for the actual work session.

Every week they would create the plot for 18 minutes of animation, most recently one episode of *Tennessee Tuxedo* (9:00) and two episodes of the *The Hunter* (4:30), then each would go back home with the outlines and write the actual scripts, including all the dialogue and all the line-by-line video instructions. The first order of business every week was to go over each completed script, discussing, arguing, adding, subtracting, timing and polishing until they were both satisfied that it was as good as it could be. Sometimes everything went smoothly and they were through with the scripts in an hour or so. Sometimes it took all morning. Only then did they move on to plotting the next episodes. By that time the

Chet's red TR-3. You had to shout to talk in it.

room was filled with papers, yellow legal pads, full ashtrays and a miasma of cigarette smoke.

Lunchtime.

They would gather up all the papers, pads, notebooks, cigarettes and, still talking, move the whole kit-n-kaboodle to their table in the dining room, cover the crisp white tablecloth with all this junk and continue working. Lunch was always the same - three martinis and a double shrimp cocktail—and arrived unbidden and on schedule.

The first martinis arrived as soon as they sat down. They were vodka martinis. Gin was preferred, but they were driving and, if stopped, the odor of vodka would be less noticeable (hopefully). They also preferred their martinis straight-up, but ordered these on-the-rocks for a very practical reason: Both men were inclined to talk with their hands and when carried away in a burst of creativity, would wave their arms about to illustrate a piece of action. Under such circumstances, the tall, stemmed, traditional martini glasses were a hazard and could be knocked over very easily, spilling precious vodka on valuable papers. Also, these tall glasses required a certain amount of elegance and concentration when drinking. You had to be careful and look attentively at what you were doing. The short, stubby rock glasses could be grasped in a fist and sipped without looking, while the drinker pounded the table or wrote down a particularly hilarious bit of business.

The second martinis would arrive just as the first were being finished. These were consumed in a more leisurely fashion. The third arrived with the shrimp cocktails. The shrimp, too, had a practical side. In addition to being delicious, they could be dipped and eaten with one hand, leaving the other hand free to write, thus not interrupting the serious work to be done.

This particular Wednesday, the first after Buck's meeting with Gordon Johnson, went no differently—the Danish and coffee, the review and polishing of the scripts, the start of two new plot outlines—until it was time for lunch. That was when Chet changed the schedule.

"All right, enough of this crap," he said, as soon as the martinis had arrived and they had taken a sip. "We can get back to the plotting later. Right now I want to know why you keep smiling like an idiot every time I mention your meeting with Gordon."

Buck turned up his hands. "I thought we ought to get finished with the 'must work' first."

Table in the 1812 House dining room.

"To hell with that. We're close enough. Let me grin, too."

Buck laughed and nodded. "Okay." He took another sip.

"Is it those damn educational consultants?" Chet asked. "Has Gordon finally got them off our backs?"

Concerned about critics because *Tennessee Tuxedo* was their first educational series, General Mills had hired two educational consultants to read and comment on *Tennessee* story summaries and scripts. "I think that's going to get better now," said Buck. "Your letter about building log cabins really did a job on those guys. Gordon says they ought to leave us alone for a while now…but that's not the news."

"So what is?"

Buck told him, laid it out almost verbatim: The Mills' need for two new series to begin in the fall of 1964, the freedom to come up with whatever they liked in terms of story and characters, the competition with Ward and Scott, the need for haste because of the revised network schedules, all of it—almost everything Gordon had passed on.

"Terrific," said Chet immediately. "That means a new series way ahead of any hope we had."

"Absolutely. *And* we get a chance to prove once and for all that we're hotter than Ward and Scott."

"It's about time," said Chet. He lifted his glass, and Buck did the same. "Here's to us." They clinked glasses, drained them, and then held up the empties for their waitress to see.

Buck said, "Gordon wants to meet with us in four weeks to see where we are."

"What do we need to have by then?"

"Just the concept, but pretty well developed." I think we need at least a script outline and thumbnail character summaries."

"That shouldn't be any problem, right?"

Buck laughed. "Piece of cake."

The owner's redheaded niece, somewhere in her early twenties, arrived with the second martinis. When she had left, Chet said, "And the kind of series—the subject matter—that's wide open, huh? No dos, don'ts, and mustn'ts?"

"Wide open. All we have to do is come up with a super series and—" Buck broke off and snapped his fingers. "No, no, I forgot. There is one limitation."

Chet froze with his glass halfway to his lips. "Uh-oh. What?"

"Stay away from frogs."

"What the hell does that mean?"

"Ward and Scott have a head start on us, and the star character in their series will be a frog."

"A *frog?*"

Buck nodded.

"What does the frog do?"

"If Gordon knows, he didn't tell me."

"Did you ask him?"

"No. To tell you the truth, I figured Gordon was already talking out of school by mentioning the frog."

Chet suddenly grinned. "You know what that means don't you?"

"What?"

"Ward and Scott have the jump on us."

They laughed together, then Buck said. "The first thing we want to do is decide on the *type* of series we want. Let's figure on each of us having four or five ideas when we meet next week. Then we'll narrow the list down to two or three and start fleshing out before we settle on one."

"Sounds good. Y'know I'm really excited about squaring off with Ward and Scott."

Buck agreed. "We'll show those guys what competition is all about."

"And no ground rules. I like that. The sky's the limit. It reminds me of a story my Uncle Charlie told me when I was a kid. He said that one year in college he took a course in astronomy. Sat in class a whole year while the professor talked about the sun and the moon and the stars. Never a quiz, never a midterm. Nothing. Then at the end of the year came the Final Exam. The professor came into the room and said, 'Gentlemen, write down all you know about the sun, all you know about the moon, all you know about the stars and then you may go'."

Buck laughed. "Exactly. That's it for us: Just sit down and write the best damn cartoon series in the history of television, and then you may go. Simple."

"Yeah, simple. Anything goes."

"Anything," Buck corrected him, "except frogs."

One day in the not-too-distant future, that single limitation would result in a portion of *The Underdog Show* that would puzzle many viewers for years and years.

"Look! Up in the sky. It's a plane...

It's a bird!

It's a frog!

A *frog?*"

"Not plane, nor bird, nor even frog.

It's just little ole me, Underdog!"

But right now, that memorable bit of television was several deep pitfalls away.

Five

What an opportunity! What a *great* opportunity! That's how Buck and Chet felt as they drove home from the 1812 House. This new series assignment was going to be right down the middle of the alley - a strike. They were sure of that.

They worked unusually hard that week, harder than they had in a long time. They completed the *Tennessee* and *Hunter* scripts in half the usual time and moved onto the new series ideas – "super" ideas, as demanded by Gordon.

And then, the unexpected happened. Once again, a signpost was raised letting it be known that this new series, and the road to it, would not be like anything they had ever encountered before. Independently (Buck and Chet did not speak by phone that week), their attitude toward this new assignment changed, changed completely. Positives turned to negatives. Every good point became a bad one. It was amazing. In less than seven days, the positive fact that this General Mills contest was "wide open" turned into the negative fact that they had no guidelines. The positive fact that the contest gave them an opportunity to prove they were the creative equals of Ward and Scott became the negative fact that Ward's popularity among the General Mills "judges" would make it impossible for Buck and Chet to get a fair shake. In short, this great opportunity became a tremendous problem.

Of course, this is not something you would have realized if you judged by the way Buck and Chet acted when they arrived at the 1812 House Wednesday morning; not when they had coffee and Danish or even when they revised and touched-up the *Tennessee* and *Hunter* scripts and plotted

27

new ones in the motel room. Although they were both somewhat sub-dued during all this, that was not unusual. They had worked together long enough and through enough (family problems, in-law problems, IRS problems, investment problems) that no hale-and-hearty camouflage was necessary between them. So they finished their script work and then adjourned for lunch.

"I know," said the owner's niece the moment they were seated in the dining room. "Two vodka martinis on the rocks with an olive."

"*Two* olives," said Chet with deadly seriousness, "but put the olives on the side so they don't steal room from the vodka."

The redhead laughed. "I'll tell the bartender, but I think he already knows."

When she had gone, Buck opened his notebook and removed a page, handing it to Chet. "The new series," he said flatly. "Here are some ideas I came up with."

Chet took the page, put it down to get his own sheet from his brief-case, and handed it to Buck. "And mine," he said.

They read these show ideas quickly. There were nine in all, and they covered a lot of territory in terms of types and time.

CALIFORNIA RED LIGHT: A combination live and animation series built around games kids love to play, plus comedy adventures. Use different live-action games as frameworks and springboards for 9-minute (or shorter) animated stories, two or three per half-hour. Use exciting kid games like "Kick the Can," "California," "Red Light," "Red Rover, Red Rover," etc.

THE HATFIELDS AND MCCOYS: All animation. An action-packed kind of variety show with the famous feud being the thread which neatly holds together a vast collection of stories, gags, songs, explosions, etc. Could make great use of old vaudeville routines (cleaned up, of course). This could be all adults, all kids or some of both. All kids would probably be best.

MEN OF THE ALAMO: A live, old-time narrator tells stories about the men who died at the Alamo. Each show opens with the Alamo battle (in animation) and includes quick cuts from one hero to another as they fight the Mexicans. There will be Crockett, Bowie, etc. Stirring music in the background. Then we interrupt this animated battle for the live narrator who tells an adventure and comedy story about what happened in the *childhood* of one of these Alamo heroes – Crockett, for example. So we have animated stories of these heroes when they were growing up. Narrator's voice will keep the action going.

MACDONALD'S MARAUDERS: A comedy combination of animated people and animals. (Yes, we can use the music and effects of "Old MacDonald Had a Farm.") Farmer MacDonald is a mean old man who captures a group of animals that have been stealing from his garden and chicken coop. He puts them in his strongest fenced-in area under the less-than-watchful eyes of his stupid helper. Instead of trying to escape, the animals, led by Farley (the fox), work out a life of splendor and ease inside the fence, even managing to help the animals outside by tipping them off about MacDonald's next produce shipment, his plan to cut down trees, etc. Plenty of room for some funny plotting.

IF I WERE HUMPHREY BOGART: Big ratings grabber, this is an animated story of a kid who wants to be just like Bogart. He wears a trench coat and hat and tries to imitate the actor, although not very well. Against the advice of his best friend (a member of the young Bogie's gang when he needs one), the kid keeps getting involved in private-eye plots with real robbers, swindlers, etc. The kicker here is that at important moments of decision in the stories, we will cut to a still of the real Bogart and have the next line delivered with a perfect Bogart imitation, and the lips on that still photograph will move in sync with the words.

COMEDY CREATORS: An all-animation series where two Otters confront a TV network programming boss and convince him that the fault with his kid show, *Uncle Don's Animal Puppets* (ratings have been terrible) is that *people* are writing the animal jokes and routines and cartoons, and they know nothing about animal humor. The Otters do, they insist. The programming boss gives the Otters a chance – an office and three months to make good. They go to work for Uncle Don, an aging comic who turns out to be a tyrant and doesn't like the idea one bit of having animals write the material for his show. So the

Otters' jobs are constantly in danger. We can have fun both at the office and at the Otters' home. Plenty of plots and plenty of laughs.

PHIL FERRET: An all-animation series based on history, but this show truly brings history to life. No dull documentary handling here. Our hero, Phil Ferret, is able to ferret out all the exciting moments in American history. And we give those moments tremendous suspense: Will the plans for the Boston Tea Party be found out in advance? Will the participants be caught? How can Phil help? Will he be able to get the lanterns to the North Church in time for Paul Revere to use as a signal? Will he be able to sneak through enemy lines with a message that could save Nathan Hale from the hangman's noose? Done the way we can do it, this could get both great ratings and reviews. (There will be no historical distortions here as in shows like Terrytoons' *Hector Heathcote*.)

TOM BROWN, SUPERSTAR: All animation. Stories of young athletes have always fascinated kids, yet no kid TV series has ever taken advantage of this. Our show will. Tom Brown excels at sports, but he is no nasty wise guy. He is a class officer and other kids look to him for leadership. Adults turn to him for advice about other kids and their problems. Tom's adventures often involve sporting contests, but he has many other interests as well. For example, Tom's work with the police to catch crooks makes him almost miss today's important football game. The team travels to various towns to play ball, so we have a variety of locations. Unlimited possibilities.

THE SECOND GREATEST SHOW ON EARTH: Great title. All animation. Series will revolve around a second-place circus, always trying to be number one. We meet the entire circus family and get involved in their comedy adventures. The "family" includes a number of different animals who are trapeze artists, clowns, jugglers, lion tamers (that's funny already), whatever. Appeal for both sexes and room for every circus plot ever seen anywhere. Hot one.

THE EMPIRE STATE BUILDING IS ALIVE!: All animation. Three animals (say, a Raccoon, a Possum and a Skunk who act much like the Three Stooges) get jobs as a cleanup crew in the Empire State Building. This involves them in a wide variety of comedy adventures with people in the many offices. When our three heroes find big trouble, they get help from an unexpected source – the Building. It turns out the Empire State Building is *alive*. It gets angry or happy, laughs and shakes, sometimes with amazing results. *Empire* helps the kids solve any great problems they face, helping them in a very unique way. Wow!

By the time Buck and Chet had finished reading these ideas, their martinis had arrived. Chet took a sip of his drink, put the sheet of paper on his briefcase and said, "Good stuff. I like them all."

Buck nodded and put down the page he was holding. "Yours, too. Great possibilities."

Their comments had been perfunctory, with little or no expression. But now, Buck added concern to his voice as he said, "They're *too* good, if you ask me. And I think that's a problem."

Chet jumped at this. "How? How do you mean?" he asked quickly. "How is it a problem?"

"We could use any one of these ideas for this…this contest we're in. Oh, maybe we'd have to toss out anything that had live-action. I think Gordon – the Mills, too – wants animation only. But except for that, any one of these ideas could be a knockout series for General Mills."

Chet was nodding, moving his head up and down as if it were on a spring. "Absolutely. That's absolutely right. And what makes it worse is that we could come up with fifty more that are just as great."

"No doubt about it," said Buck, seeing that Chet had caught his point. "And where does that leave us? How the hell are we supposed to make a choice about which idea to go with?"

"No guidelines. We've got no direction here at all."

Buck pointed at the two sheets of paper with their series ideas. "We've got shows involving everything from a circus to a private-eye, and that doesn't even scratch the surface. We could come up with a great idea for almost any occupation in the yellow pages, and we could place it in any time from one million B.C. to one million A.D. and locate it anywhere on earth."

"Or the universe. Anywhere in the universe."

Buck nodded. "The assignment sounded great at first. Wide open."

"Anything goes."

"Yeah. Anything but frogs."

Chet's eyes narrowed. "Do you think Gordon meant something special by that?"

"What do you mean?"

"Was he trying to tip us off to something more than just not to use frogs? I mean, maybe he was trying to give us direction about the kind of character."

Buck shrugged. "I don't see how that would work. He's just saying Ward and Scott are using a frog on their show for their main character. So we should go with some other kind of creature."

Chet nodded and pointed his finger at Buck. "That's my point: some other kind of 'creature.' Does that mean he doesn't want us using characters that are human?"

Buck thought about this as he took a swallow of his martini. In a moment, he shrugged and said, "I think Gordon would probably feel safer if we went with animals – or insects or reptiles. Anything but humans. And why wouldn't he? We've done damn well with them as our lead characters so far. But if we came up with something red hot – dynamite – that had human characters in the lead, I honestly don't think it would matter." He nodded. "And that's the problem. Except for steering clear of frogs and sticking with animation, I don't think it would make a damn bit of difference *what* kind of characters we came up with – or what occupation or anything else."

Chet was nodding again. "That's where they stiffed us. If you're setting out to dig for gold, it's not a map of the world you want. What good is that going to do?"

"None. And we've got nobody to talk to, nobody to try and pump." Buck smiled sarcastically. "You can bet your frigging shirt that Ward has already tapped into somebody at the Mills, and they're going over one by one the likes and dislikes of every guy who's going to have a vote on these new shows."

Chet took a sip of his drink. "If that's true, maybe it means we ought to try and come up with something like a frog." He stopped and turned up his hands. "That sounds weird, doesn't it? Can you imagine anybody telling Jay, 'Here's the inside poop: We've got three guys who like frogs.'" He laughed.

Buck laughed with him. "And even if they did, how could we come up with something *like* a frog? What the hell is there that's *like* a frog?"

"Maybe a tadpole."

"Or an eel or a snake."

"Yuk."

"My sentiments exactly," said Buck. "If there's somebody at the Mills who has a thing about frogs, there's not much we can do about it."

"Maybe use buckshot."

"What?"

Chet smiled. "Remember that old Mark Twain story about somebody filling the frog with buckshot so he'd lose the jumping contest? Maybe that's what we ought to do with Ward's frog."

"Not his frog. Our only chance would be to fill *Ward* with buckshot."

Chet laughed. "Now, now, don't get carried away. It's only a contest."

Their second drink arrived. They thanked the waitress (always more profusely after each drink) and when she had gone, Buck said, "I guess what worries me most about all this is the fact that Ward's so damned popular with everybody at the Mills. Maybe he causes some problems with scripts, but that only makes him seem more like a creative genius."

"Oh, sure. That's how it works."

Buck sighed. "Of course, it's more than that with Jay. He's a very, very creative guy. His stuff is tremendous."

Chet nodded. "Bullwinkle is great."

"Yeah, but he was doing terrific stuff long before that. His *Crusader Rabbit* was one of the first cartoon shows made for TV."

Chet shrugged. "I never saw it."

"Special. Very special. So there's no argument about his talent, but the problem is, I'm afraid a lot of the guys will prejudge his stuff. If it's us versus Ward and Scott, we may be doomed even before they see what we've got to offer."

"Right. They took our first series because they needed to give Ward and Scott some competition. They took our second because Ward rejected the idea of doing something educational. But if we go head-to-head with him, what chance have we got...no matter *what* we come up with?"

"And it gets worse," said Buck. "If the guys at the Mills start out ready to make Jay the winner no matter what the shows are, they'll be looking for ways to knock our stuff. They'll pounce on every possible negative they can find. And you know what that means. They'll not only choose Ward's show over ours, but because they've peed all over our idea, they won't even accept it for ABC."

Chet nodded. "And after all that work, our series will end up in the garbage can."

Buck leaned back in his chair, sipping his martini. "We need to figure some way to create guidelines for ourselves," he shrugged. "With *King Leonardo*, we just did what we wanted to do."

"Sure. It wasn't a contest. We were the only ones presenting. And anyhow, we didn't have anything to lose."

"And with *Tennessee*," said Buck, "we knew they wanted a show that would educate while it entertained. We had guidelines."

"But with this one, we've got nothing. Absolute zero. Zip. And we sure as hell *do* have something to lose. This just happens to be the only job we've got."

"Which is why we have to figure some way to devise guidelines that will give us an edge."

Chet shook his head. "There isn't any way. We've been over everything we know. We're licked before we start." He held up his left hand and pulled down one finger at a time. "First, we've got no idea what kind of show would be a winner. Second, we've got nobody on the inside to tip us off. Third, we know that most of the guys at the Mills think Ward is a creative genius, so he has the edge going in. And, fourth, the only guideline we have is not to use a frog because Jay got there first." He dropped his hand and picked up his martini. "I rest my case. We're up the creek."

"Okay," said Buck, "we've got to figure a way to get a paddle."

"To hell with a paddle. We need a boat, and a motor would be nice, too." Chet shook his head again. "I'm telling you, there's no way to win this thing. It sounded great last week, but not anymore. We haven't got a prayer."

Buck squinted his eyes and slowly lifted his hand to point at Chet.

"What?" asked Chet. "Why are you pointing at me?"

Buck smiled. "Don't those words sound familiar?"

"What words?"

"The ones you just said: 'We haven't got a prayer.' They're the same words you used the day I came to you in your office at DFS, the same words you used when I first told you we ought to create a cartoon series. You said: 'We haven't got a prayer.'"

Now Chet returned the smile. "And I was right," he said, laughing softly. "We didn't have a prayer then either."

Six

It was May 13, 1959. Buck and Chet were both working at Dancer-Fitzgerald-Sample (DFS), a top-twenty advertising agency at 347 Madison Avenue in New York City. Clients included many major companies, such as Proctor and Gamble, Sterling Drug, General Mills, Corn Products-Best Foods and Falstaff Beer. Buck was an Account Executive on General Mills products. Chet was a Creative Director, lending his talents to almost all of the agency's top accounts. Buck and Chet had worked together many times, primarily on Cheerios and O-Celo Sponges.

At a little before noon on May 13, Buck left his office on the seventh floor and climbed one flight of stairs. Those who knew him well would probably have been surprised by the expression on his face, a strange combination of puzzlement and excitement.

Crossing the yellow linoleum-tiled expanse, Buck waved at Chet's secretary, a young blonde woman somewhat overweight, then poked his head inside Chet's office. "You busy?" Buck asked.

Dropping his pencil on the yellow pad where he had been writing, Chet turned up his hands. "Nothing that can't wait."

Buck sat down in the chair facing Chet's desk. This was a large corner office, bright with two windows, and tastefully decorated in modernistic décor, including wall-to-wall cabinets, a full-length couch and two chairs.

"What's up?" Chet asked. "You look like you swallowed a canary...maybe a cross-eyed canary."

"I just had the damnedest conversation with Gordon."

Chet laughed. "What else is new? Was he chewing paper?"

Buck nodded. "Like it was going out of style." Gordon Johnson had a

Chet's office at DFS where Buck first broached the idea of creating a cartoon series.

habit of tearing off small pieces of paper, usually the bottom of some memo on his desk, folding this carefully time and time again until it was bite-sized, then popping it into his mouth and chewing as if it were gum. He never explained why and no one had the nerve to ask him, afraid it might sound as if they were criticizing this strange habit. There was conjecture that he used the paper to help him cut down on smoking, but if that was the idea, it did not seem to work very well. He smoked like a chimney.

Chet said, "One of these days we ought to tell him he could double his pleasure with Double Mint Gum."

"*You* tell him, not me. Anywho, he was chewing paper and talking a mile-a-minute. He's uptight about the cartoon show."

"What cartoon show?"

"The only one General Mills has—*Rocky and His Friends*. Haven't you seen it?"

Chet nodded. "Oh, sure. The squirrel and the moose. I saw the pilot, and we're doing some special Cheerios commercials for it. I think it's funny."

"So do I. And so does Gordon."

"So why is he uptight?"

"He's got a problem with the creators of the series." The phone rang, but Chet left it up to his secretary to answer, so Buck went on. "General Mills is paying for this assembly line in Mexico – Gamma Products; peons painting *Rocky* cels before they're photographed for animation. With all these people on the payroll, the Mills can't afford to have the assembly line shut down."

Chet's secretary came in. "It's Mr. Fitzgerald's office. They want you there at 4:30 for a meeting about the new L&M campaign. Is that all right?"

Irritably, Chet said, "It wasn't supposed to be until tomorrow." He shrugged and sighed. "But tell them it's okay." He nodded. "4:30."

When his secretary had gone, Chet lifted a pack of L&M's on his desk and offered the pack to Buck.

"No, thanks."

Chet took one of the cigarettes and lit it with the silver lighter on his desk. "That means I'll be late getting home again." He shook his head. "It gets worse and worse with this client. They push up the meetings, back down on what they say, change their minds quicker than their underwear, and never say what they mean or mean what they say. It's driving me up the wall." He had told Buck many times about his problems with the L&M account.

Buck said lightly, "But it's a prestige account, my friend."

"You know what you can do with that prestige…Forget L&M. You were talking about Gordon's problem with *Rocky*."

Buck nodded. "I was saying that General Mills can't afford to have the animation assembly line in Mexico shut down. It costs too much and, also, we've got a tight delivery schedule for *Rocky* shows; get behind and we won't be able to supply ABC with new shows on schedule."

Chet blew smoke into the air. "So what's the problem?"

"The creators of the series. They're the problem. Jay Ward and Bill Scott. Some of their *Rocky* scripts have lines that General Mills – ABC, too – don't think are appropriate for kids. They'd be fine if this were a show in adult time but we're talking kids. So far, Gordon's usually been able to convince Jay he should make changes, but it's getting tougher and tougher…and taking a helluva lot of Gordon's time."

"What kind of lines are you talking about?"

Buck thought a moment, then said, "The one I remember best was where Bullwinkle is doing his 'Mr. Know-It-All' character, and he tells Rocky that the way to start a fire out in the woods is to rub two Boy Scouts together."

Chet grimaced. "*Rub two Boy Scouts together?* My God, the Mills must have flipped." Chet was well-aware that critics were already at work trying to control the content of television programming for kids. "Concerned parents," afraid TV was corrupting their children, were forming groups to apply pressure at the marketplace. A company like General Mills, trying to sell their cereals to parents as well as children, could not afford to offend adults, and there was no doubt that adults would hear the *Rocky* lines, especially in these days when a single TV set was the norm for a home. What the kids heard, Mom heard too.

"There have been too many lines like that," said Buck, "and while the arguments about them are going on, Ward often shuts down the inking and painting in Mexico. The Gamma assembly line goes bam! Everything stops. Which means that the people on the line are getting paid for doing nothing. That's bad enough, but think what stoppages like that will mean after the show goes on the air in November. Gamma's supposed to be cranking out a full show every week. If they shut down, what does ABC run in the *Rocky* time slot, reruns of *The Lone Ranger?*"

Chet nodded. "That's a bitch." He ground out his cigarette in the green ashtray, then lifted his pencil and began tapping it lightly on the yellow pad. He had begun to wonder why Buck was going into such detail about this cartoon show problem. At first it had seemed that Buck was only sharing his own sense of confusion, but that did not seem to be the case. Was there some particular kind of help he wanted? "So what's the upshot?" Chet asked, tapping the pencil against the pad.

Buck did not answer directly. "They had so much trouble getting Gamma started in the first place that Gordon had to put some of his own money in there. The place was totally undercapitalized. If that assembly line shuts down, it's not just DFS and General Mills and ABC that will get hurt. Gordon can take a big hit personally."

"So, what's he want to do?"

Buck cleared his throat and leaned back in his chair. "That's the crazy part. Gordon said he wants me to find a new supplier, a new creative group."

Chet laughed. "You mean a new group to write *Rocky*?"

"No, no. Gordon can't do that. He wants a new show. He knows I've got TV production contacts, so he wants me to find a creative team with a red-hot cartoon series for Saturday morning. But, Gordon says, he wants to be sure it's a team *I* can control. If he said that once, he said it five times. 'Be sure it's a team you can control.'"

Chet frowned. "How would a new team – a new series – help the situation with Ward and Scott?"

"If General Mills buys a second series to be produced at Gamma, anytime Ward and Scott shut down their writing, Gordon can keep the assembly line going with episodes of the other series."

"Ohhhh." Chet nodded. "I get it. So you've got to find a creative team who are peddling a cartoon series. Are there a lot of them out there?"

"I don't think so. Not any that would really fit. Not in New York."

"Did you tell Gordon that?"

Buck shook his head. "I think he already knows. Los Angeles would be the logical place to dig up that kind of group. Gordon knows that." He looked directly at Chet. "So, why do you think he asked me to do it? He made it seem very, very important, and he didn't want any answer from me but, 'Sure. I'll take care of it.' Why would he ask me to do that?"

So this was it, Chet thought. Buck had told him all this because he could not understand why Gordon had given him this responsibility. Chet said, "You know Gordy. It could be that he just figures you've got such great contacts that you can find what he needs."

Buck shook his head. "I don't think that's it."

"Why not?"

"Well, even if I did, even if I could find the right creative team, how could I 'control' them?"

Chet shrugged. "Maybe with a tough contract."

Again Buck shook his head. "Contracts don't mean a thing if you can hold up an assembly line. I bring in a new group, they seem beholden to me, then quick-as-a-wink they decide since they're a creative group, they ought to side with the other creative group. Bang! Gordon would be right back where he is now."

Chet turned up his hands. "So it looks hopeless."

"Not necessarily. The truth is, I don't think Gordon *wants* me to find a creative group."

"So why did he ask you?"

Now Buck smiled and winked. "I don't think he wants me to find a group. I think he wants me to *form* one...and that's what I'm doing right now. I want us—you and me..." he pointed at himself and then Chet, ". . . to create a new cartoon series."

Chet's eyes flew open, and the pencil in his hand broke in half as if it had a life of its own. "Have you lost your mind?" he asked, dropping the pieces of pencil. "What the hell do we know about creating a cartoon series?"

Buck stood up, walked to the door and closed it quietly, then returned to the chair. "Don't you understand?" He waved his hands excitedly. "We've already got half the battle won. Gordon is the guy we'd have to sell, and he's asking me to form a group."

"Why? Why you?"

"Because he trusts me. And because he knows I want to do something more creative. And he also knows I want to get the hell out of New York."

Chet was surprised. "You could leave New York if you make this work?"

"Why not? Ward and Scott are in California, for Christ's sake. We could move anywhere. How many opportunities will we get to do that?"

There was fire in Chet's eyes for a moment, but it faded quickly. He flopped his hands forward. "We don't know the first thing about writing a cartoon series."

"The hell we don't. Who created the Cheerios Kid?"

"I did," said Chet, "but he's...he's a commercial character, not part of a show."

The Cheerios Kid was internationally recognized as one of the greatest selling tools in the history of kid advertising. Buck said, "He has adventures, doesn't he?"

"Sure. Sure he does. He has adventures, but they're only thirty seconds long, followed by another thirty seconds of hard sell for Cheerios. That's a pretty short program. Are they scheduling thirty-second shows these days?"

"It's the same principle."

"Really? How do we turn thirty seconds into thirty minutes?"

Buck shook his head. "The series aren't really thirty minutes long. There are eighteen minutes of new show material in each half-hour. The rest are commercials plus opens and closes and fillers that are basically the same in each show. And the longest piece in that eighteen minutes is only

The Cheerios Kid, a remarkable advertising creation

4 1/2 minutes long. At least that's how it is on *Rocky*, and that's how Gordon wants it in the new series." Buck winked. "And how far is a 4 1/2-minute adventure from a thirty-second one?"

Chet waved his hands back and forth in front of his face. "I don't know what you had for breakfast, but I think it gave you amnesia. The last time I looked, we both had a wife and two kids and a mortgage." He lowered his voice almost to a whisper. "And we also have damn good jobs here at the agency. As long as the bank owns my house, I don't think I'm going to be doing *anything* that might interrupt a steady paycheck. You hear what I'm saying?"

Chet was right about their jobs. They were both far up the executive ladder at DFS. They were well-liked, well-respected and their future prospects were bright. But as solid as their positions were, all was far from rosy with their lives.

Buck, a Southerner by birth, felt strangled by the city and also by some of his in-laws. In truth, the problem with his in-laws was seriously jeopardizing Buck's marriage. He had recently moved his family from Hicksville, Long Island to Hartsdale, New York, so that occasionally weekends might be spent without the inclusion of his wife's family. But two of those family members, bothered not at all by the distance between Hicksville and Hartsdale, continued to arrive at Buck's doorstep promptly every Saturday morning. More distance seemed the only way to change this situation.

Chet, too, had dreams of leaving the city (becoming a "gentleman farmer," perhaps), but his main source of unhappiness lay with the agency having chosen him as the Creative Director for L&M cigarettes. Although he smoked (everyone on the account had to smoke, and the only brand they dared choose was L&M), Chet hated having to create ads which might encourage people to smoke or to smoke more often. Having been aware since 1954 of the connection between cigarettes and cancer, Chet found slogans such as "Reach for A Lucky Instead of A Sweet" especially repugnant, and he hated having to suggest that filters were beneficial since he knew that, in fact, they only caused people to inhale more deeply and hold the smoke in longer.

In addition, every tobacco medical study that appeared, always tightening the link between cigarettes and cancer and cigarettes and death, caused increasing panic among the tobacco executives responsible for advertising. They worried over every word in an ad, changed their minds endlessly, blamed the agency for errors which were actually theirs and, in general, simply ran scared. Writing advertising copy could be fun, but not when you had to worry more about pleasing the client than getting it right.

Still, as unhappy as Chet was with his job, his first concern was his wife and two sons. "You pay off my mortgage," he told Buck now, "and *then* we can talk about putting my job in jeopardy."

"But that's just it," said Buck, lowering his voice to match Chet's, as if they were in danger of being overheard. "We don't have to jeopardize our jobs. We can create this show without anybody knowing, and then see what happens. If the show sells, we're in business, *big* business - a million-dollar contract. Enough to let us walk away from DFS. And if the show isn't bought by the Mills, all we've wasted is time. That's all. Time."

Chet started to answer, but his intercom suddenly buzzed, and they both jumped as if caught in the midst of a robbery. It was Chet's secretary telling him she was leaving for lunch.

Putting down the phone, Chet sighed and leaned back in his chair. "You were saying we could do this without anybody knowing. I was about to laugh at that when the buzzer scared the pee out of me, and that just goes to show what it would be like trying to create a cartoon series in secret. Especially since I don't know a frigging thing about creating such a series."

Buck shook his head and pointed at himself. "I do know about cartoons. I'm the one who has to revise the *Rocky* format and make it work when changes are needed. I've even presented a couple of problem episodes at the Mills. I know what we need to do. And we can do it. You know how fast we work as a team. We're hot. And we can create anywhere. We'll meet where nobody will know about it; create this series without a soul knowing about it until we're ready. Then we'll get somebody to front the sale."

"And if anybody discovers we're involved, we're out on the street."

Buck waved a finger back and forth. "Not so, not so. damn near everybody in this agency—in every agency—is trying to do something else, trying to get out of advertising. They're working on a book or a play or a movie—anything to get out of this business."

"But that's different. Sure, we've all tried to peddle stories or poems or whatever. But this is a different kettle of fish. We could be into conflict here. It could get very, very sticky."

Buck shook his head. "There's no conflict here. The interest is all the same. General Mills has a big problem and maybe we can take care of it. Maybe we can keep that Gamma assembly line running so that the Mills gets cartoon shows at a great price, far cheaper than they could get in Hollywood. We help our clients get the finest and most cost-efficient programs possible for their commercials. That's what we do."

Chet frowned, considering this a moment, then he asked, "Even if we did actually come up with a series, how would it get to Gordon? Who would show it to him - you? Certainly not me."

"We bring in another partner, a front man."

Chet looked skeptical. "And right away, you're blowing it with Gordon. How can you keep anybody in line that we bring in?"

"Simple. We form a company, and you and I always have the controlling block of stock. It's that simple."

For a moment Chet seemed to waver, but then shook his head firmly.

"The work you've done with *Rocky* doesn't mean you know how to create a series. And I sure as hell don't." Again he shook his head. "We wouldn't have a prayer."

The words seemed to leave no room for argument, yet Buck was not ready to give up. This was a once-in-a-lifetime opportunity. Sure, he could try it with someone else, but that thought took all the wind out of his sails. From the moment Gordon had given him the assignment, working with Chet had been in Buck's mind. There had to be some way to bring him around. Now, Buck asked, "Can we have lunch? I want to keep talking about this."

Seven

Still arguing animatedly, waving their hands like bandleaders, Buck and Chet walked to the Teheran, a two-story, off-Fifth Avenue restaurant full of white-clothed tables, tweedy tan carpeting, reasonable prices and an excellent Zabaglione dessert. Seated at a small corner table, they ordered martinis, and—amazingly—even before they had each finished two of these, Chet made a complete about-face, agreeing to work with Buck on creating a cartoon series and getting it sold to General Mills.

Why? What was it that made Chet accept the gamble he had rejected so adamantly only a short while earlier? Well, this many years later, even Chet is not certain of the answer. Maybe in part it was the pleasant atmosphere of the Teheran. Maybe in part it was the silver oratory flowing from Buck's lips. Maybe in part it was the silver bullets (martinis) flowing from the bar and maybe in part, probably the most important "maybe" of all, it was the phone call Chet received just before they left DFS for the restaurant.

That call had come from the L&M Account Supervisor, and it had nothing to do with Chet's 4:30 meeting about a new campaign. Instead, for the sixth time in only 10 days, Chet was advised that L&M had asked for still more changes in an ad which was part of the current campaign, an ad which Chet had personally created. And to make matters worse, Chet learned that the Account Supervisor had already approved the changes without even consulting him.

Slamming down the phone, he had said to Buck, "If I see that damn ad in a magazine, I won't even recognize the piece of crap. It's had more changes than Christine Jorgenson." (This was a reference to the woman who had been surgically created from a man.)

The memory of that phone call had stayed with Chet as they walked to the Teheran, as they drank their martinis, and as Buck spoke again and again of the "freedom" they could enjoy by becoming an independent creative team. And so, for whatever reason, Chet finally said yes. He and Buck were ready to try their hand at creating a cartoon series.

But where to begin?

"Don't look at me," said Chet after they had placed their food order. "You're going to have to lead this parade. I don't even *watch* cartoons." He leaned across the table. "In fact, don't let it get around, but I don't watch much commercial television at all. Maybe a little *Playhouse 90*, otherwise, we like educational TV."

"Don't worry about it. I love to watch cartoons. *Huckleberry Hound* is my new favorite." He smiled. "We'll make a great team. You can supply the highbrow, head laughs, and I'll supply the lowbrow, belly laughs. Perfect."

"When do you watch that show?" Chet asked. "I mean *Huckleberry Hound*. Is it on Saturday mornings?"

Buck shook his head. "It's syndicated, not network; comes on twice during the week. Six o'clock, I think. You can catch it if you get out of the office on time."

"Tell that to L&M. What about *Rocky*? Will that be Saturday morning?"

Again Buck shook his head. "No."

"But it's network, isn't it?"

"Yeah, but it's ABC. They're still way behind CBS and NBC—don't have much of a Saturday morning line-up. So *Rocky* will be weekly afternoons, like *Huck*."

"But the new series Gordon wants will be on Saturday morning?"

"Right," said Buck. "Probably on NBC. Which means our series will be in color. Won't that be terrific?"

"*Our* series? You're already positive we'll have one?"

"Of course."

"And it'll be applauded by General Mills?"

"No doubt about it. We're going to bowl the Mills over."

"Amazing," said Chet sarcastically. And then, as their balding waiter arrived with their meal, Chet pointed at Buck and told the waiter, "Be sure and give this man plenty of food. I think he's intoxicated."

The waiter laughed and so did Buck. "We'll see," he said. "We'll see."

It would not be possible for them to leap directly into the creation of the series. Although time was of the essence, there was a job that had to be done first: research. If they wanted to develop a TV cartoon series that would "bowl the Mills over," then they had damn well better know exactly what kind of kid shows had already been on the air and how they had rated, especially on Saturday morning. This was job #1.

They expected that finding this information would be a snap. Just go to the bookstore or perhaps to the library and get a book, something like *The History of Saturday Morning* or *The History of Kid TV*. Wrong. Dead wrong. There was no such book. Too few years had passed since the beginning of programming. They would have to dig out their own history.

First, they visited a very large second-hand bookstore where they were able to purchase most issues of *TV Guide* dating all the way back to 1952. Second, they visited DFS's Media Department, being very careful (probably unnecessarily so) to do nothing which might raise awkward questions. They were here to look at A.C. Nielsen ratings for kid TV shows.

These visits to DFS Media were always made *after* business hours. In fact, Buck and Chet made certain that all their work on the TV series, except perhaps for an occasional code word in the seventh floor men's room, was carried out either on weekends or outside the DFS 9 to 5 work brackets. "We may be nuts," said Chet, "but we're honest nuts."

What they soon learned was that the history of kid TV did not have a great deal to offer in the way of advice. What would soon become known as "Saturday Morning TV," the networks' major homeland for children's programming, had not come into being at that time (it really began with the 1960-61 season). From 1952 to 1959, more kid shows were scheduled on weekdays (mornings and afternoons) than on Saturday mornings. And Saturday morning was almost as likely to include adult programs, such as Laurel and Hardy or *Saturday Playhouse*, as it was to include kid shows.

As for the *type* of kid programming that had been scheduled over the years, both on Saturday morning and during the week, variety was the name of the game. There were live people series like *Captain Kangaroo*, there were film people series like *Fury* and *Sky King*, there were puppet series like *Howdy Doody* and *Kukla, Fran and Ollie*, there were pieced-together theater cartoon series like *Mighty Mouse* and *Heckle and Jeckle* with live hosts, there were stop-motion series like *Gumby*, there were *very* limited animation series like *Tom Terrific* and *Clutch Cargo*, there were less limited but much repeated cartoon series like *Crusader Rabbit*. The only new animation series which had premiered on Saturday morning was Hanna-Barbera's *Ruff and Reddy* (Dec. 14, 1957), but although it rated extremely well, it was not a complete animation series since it required a live host (Jimmy Blaine).

When Buck and Chet first discussed this particular piece of information, they were having lunch in Grand Central Station's Oyster Bar restaurant. "Do you realize," Buck asked excitedly, "that if we bring this off, we'll have the first all-animation series ever to debut on Saturday morning?"

Chet nodded, his mouth a straight line. "And do you realize that if you find pearls in all those oysters you're eating, you'll be worth a fortune? But I wouldn't bank on it."

Obviously, he was still not convinced they could do this.

As more and more rating information was accumulated, several factors became clear: All other things being equal, animation almost always out-rated other program types—live-action, puppets, people films or stop-motion. But if the animation was extremely limited, like *Clutch Cargo*, or it had been repeated too many times, like *Crusader Rabbit*, ratings fell.

What most interested Buck and Chet was the fact that ratings also fell when the animation was aimed at the very young. It was clear that since the vast majority of homes had only a single television set, either adults or the older children were in control. They chose the shows, and they did not choose kiddie stuff unless that was the only show available.

"We've got to give this series some over-the-shoulder appeal," said Chet.

Buck agreed. "We'd have to do that anyway. It's adults who'll buy the series, not kids. And I've watched them with *Rocky*. If they don't laugh, they don't think it's funny for kids, and they won't buy it."

"It's the same with kid commercials. Nobody asks themselves if it's funny to kids. They ask if it's funny to *them*."

"So we have to give our show a second level of comedy. It has to work for the little kids but have an appeal for the older ones, too."

Their research was not complete. Not yet. If they were going to create a cartoon series built around animal characters – and Buck was certain this is what Gordon wanted – then they wanted to know all the animals that had already been used for kid TV animation and, particularly, those that had spent much time on Saturday morning.

The reason was simple: Since there were an almost unlimited number of animals to choose from for their major characters, why choose ones which had already been used?

"You know what Gordon will do," said Buck. "If he hears we've got a show about a bear, the first thing he'll say is, 'Hanna-Barbera already did that with Yogi.'"

"Yeah," said Chet, "and if he'd been around when Leonardo da Vinci was about to paint the Mona Lisa, he'd probably have said, 'Forget it, Leonardo. Somebody already painted a woman.'"

So for the main characters on their cartoon series, they agreed to avoid mice and cats as well as magpies, kangaroos, pups, ducks, rabbits, tigers, pigs, squirrels, moose, woodpeckers and alligators.

They had their research now. No more procrastinating, no more putting off the inevitable. It was time to bear down on creating that series, and this meant intense collaboration. But where? Oh, they could have worked after-hours in Buck or Chet's office, but they knew this would make them too nervous.

"Every time a door creaked," said Buck, "I'd have to change my shorts."

They could also have worked at one home or the other (and they did on one or two occasions), but what they needed was complete isolation, and they were not likely to find this in the midst of wives and children and pets.

They did find it, however, in a gas station. A gas station? That's right. Almost exactly halfway between Buck's home in Hartsdale and Chet's in Rockland County, they discovered a deserted gas station, all boarded up so that it looked like two giant crates nailed together. The surface surrounding the building was white gravel, not cement, and it was here that they parked their two cars early that first Saturday morning.

Chet brought his notebook and briefcase to Buck's brand new all-white Plymouth station wagon with push-button drive. "Why push-button?" Chet asked as soon as he was inside the car. "Why the hell didn't you get a shift?" Chet loved a shift.

"Grace [Buck's wife] is learning how to drive. We figured it would be easier without a clutch."

"Oh." He did not sound impressed.

"And," said Buck, "without the gearshift, you and I have a helluva lot more room to work." He waved his hand around the front seat.

The deserted gas station midway between Buck and Chet's homes which, along with Buck's Plymouth station wagon, became their first office.

Chet nodded slowly, considering this. "Yeah," he said in a moment. "A helluva lot more room."

And so it was that the new creative team found an office: a white push-button station wagon parked on the graveled surface of a deserted gas station. Here, they began searching for their first series.

Far sooner than Buck had anticipated, there was no longer any need for him to work at making Chet positive about the show. They both began having so much fun creating the characters and plots and dialogue that there was no time for misgivings. Part of the reason was the fact that their show was not just a kid show. Thanks to their research, they were creating a comedy series that would appeal to all ages. So, naturally, the series appealed to them.

Eight

It took Buck and Chet four weeks to get what they wanted: a basic storyline, character summaries and pilot script. There were wrong turns, dead ends, many revisions and then revisions upon revisions. But when all of this – all the meetings and phone calls and messages – is telescoped, this is the story behind their first series.

They began by looking for a location, a place their heroes would call home. Since they had no guidelines except the need to be original, they decided to lift from their own lives. They were in the advertising business, and this business was thought of by most everyone as a "jungle." So they would set their series in a real jungle: Africa.

They liked the idea immediately, finding it surprising that this location had not been chosen by others. All those different cartoon animals on TV, yet none of them had lived in what most people considered the home of wildlife: The jungle.

Pleased by the way advertising had led them to this location, they decided to continue with the correlation. In the jungle, who was the CEO? The king, of course. And among the animals of the jungle, which one was the king? The lion, of course. And so, the lead character, their number one star attraction, would be a royal lion.

Oops! Hold that decision. First they had to check their research to see if lions had been big on Saturday mornings. The answer was no. No Saturday morning series had starred a lion. And none on weekday afternoons or mornings either. There had been a couple of lions starring in theater short subjects, but none in a television series. The lion was a go. The King. The CEO.

Continuing the advertising corollary, what about an exec for the CEO? A right-hand man. Someone to stand between the CEO and all those who work for him – his "subjects." Could there be a more likely candidate than a skunk? Nobody argues with a skunk. He can look as small and friendly as a stuffed animal, but when he gets his back up, who dares to tangle with him? A skunk. Loyal to the throne. Ready to give his life for his King. True blue.

But wait. Hadn't there already been a skunk on TV? Wasn't there one named Pepé? No. It turned out that Pepé—Pepé Le Pew—had been the star of some theater short subjects, but he had never made it to television. Good. The King's right-hand animal would be a skunk. Together, they would be the team of good guys.

And the bad guys? Who would the villains be? Knowing that they would need a continuing plot to underpin the series, Buck and Chet decided to give their King the kind of pawn that had made such great successes of stories like "The Prisoner of Zenda," "The Man in the Iron Mask" and "The Prince and the Pauper." The King must have a lookalike. A brother. Although there would be a great resemblance, this would not be apparent usually because their character would be so different.

How? Well, the King would be regal, proud, perfectly groomed, perfectly clothed. So his brother would be…his brother would be…a beatnik! An ill-clothed, dirty, smelly, itchy, mangy-looking lion.

But a beatnik should be somewhat brainless, so if the brother is plotting against the King, where would he find the brains to plot all those plots? Who would be the brother's partner-in-crime? Who would be the one who, time and time again, nearly brings the royal reign to a rotten end? A dirty rat, that's who. A mean, ugly, tough-talking rat.

Hold it. Check the research. What about a rat as a major character on Saturday morning? No. Not there or even on weekday kid time. Plenty of mice, no rats. There were a few in comic books and theater short subjects, but none on TV. Okay, a dirty rat it was.

If there was to be a continuing effort to capture the throne from our hero King, then the throne had to be worth something. This African country had to be successful; had to have a healthy economy. Make it a "manufacturing" country. And what was the product? Hear that distant sound? Drums, of course. They manufacture drums. Bongo drums. Bongo drums in the Congo, so the country is Bongo Congo. Beautiful.

With the basic concept and major characters in place, they turned to character names and voice selections. Because Buck was the only "TV Account Executive" for General Mills, he was certain Gordon would have him present this new show to the executives in Minneapolis (assuming, of course, that Gordon liked it himself). With this in mind, voices were chosen that Buck could imitate well. A few years earlier, in another attempt to escape from the advertising business to something more creative, Buck had worked on a stand-up comedy routine which included a number of Hollywood imitations. It was some of these that Buck and Chet chose for their series.

As the voice of their powerful potentate, they chose the low-pitched gravely intonations of a wonderful character actor who had appeared in many, many movies, including *Mr. Smith Goes to Washington* and, as Friar Tuck, *The Adventures of Robin Hood*. This was Eugene Pallette, who had died five years earlier (1954). As for the King's name, hadn't they been talking recently about Leonardo da Vinci and the Mona Lisa? *Leonardo*. A very prestigious, very important name. King Leonardo. Leonardo Lion. Nice.

Actor Eugene Pallette, the voice (imitated) for King Leonardo.

For the King's right-hand animal, his most trusted Lieutenant, they chose a voice that was the epitome of dignity and steadfastness, the English-accented voice of an actor who had starred in such stalwart roles as *The Prisoner of Zenda* and in *Random Harvest*. This was Ronald Colman, who had died only the previous year (1958).

What should they name this second-in-command, this protector of the King, this valiant skunk? They decided on the highly redundant "Odie Colognie." True blue Odie.

For the beatnik brother, what better voice than that of a former prize fighter who sounded as if he had not retired from the ring soon enough and was, as a result, somewhat punch-drunk. This was "Slapsie" Maxie Rosenbloom, who, still living then, had appeared in such films as *The Amazing Dr. Clitterhouse* and *Abbott and Costello Meet the Keystone Kops*. Since the brother was mangy and itchy, they named him "Itchy Brother."

And, finally, for the dirty rat who would mastermind most of the villainy in the series, they selected the truly unique voice of Edward G. Robinson, a Hollywood superstar who had appeared in a long, long list of fine movies (and would appear in many more after 1959), yet was best remembered for his gangster boss Rico Bandello in *Little Caesar*. They named this big evil boss of Bongo Congo "Biggy Rat."

The working title for the series had been *The King and His Kingdom*. It was time to decide if this would be the final title.

"I like the redundancy and alliteration," said Buck or Chet, "but it doesn't help the characters come to life."

"How about *King Leonardo and His Kingdom*?"

"How about *King Leonardo and His Subjects*?"

A pause. "It's still not right."

And then, in a burst, "How about *King Leonardo and His* Short *Subjects*?"

They broke into laughter, not simply because they knew Odie and Biggy would be so much shorter than the King, but because the title reminded them of the recent past when movie theaters had promoted their cartoons as "short subjects." So that became the show's title: *King Leonardo and His Short Subjects*.

They decided against having the King and Odie involved in ten-part (or more) stories as Jay Ward had used for his *Crusader Rabbit* (and now for *Rocky*) and as Hanna-Barbera had used for *Ruff and Reddy*. Buck knew that such carryover stories did not allow freedom in terms of shifting

Actor Ronald Colman, the voice (imitated) chosen for true-blue Odie Colognie.

episodes around in case of a production slowdown or to take advantage of holiday episodes, etc. Instead, such continuing stories forced the network or stations to run the episodes in order. On the other hand, they did not want to do single episode stories like *Huckleberry Hound* because a continuing story encouraged kids to stay with the show for a full half-hour.

They decided to use two-part stories for the King and Odie, part one at the opening of the half-hour, part two at the close. In between, they would need two other 4+-minute episodes, each a complete story in itself and featuring subsidiary characters.

Rules about not choosing animals already used on Saturday morning did not apply to these less important characters, and the very first choice was a Southern hound who would be a private-eye ("Have Nose, Will Hunt") known only as The Hunter. He was forever chasing the wily, clever Fox who had a reputation for outlandish crimes such as stealing the Brooklyn Bridge. The Hunter's voice would be like that of Senator Claghorn, a character created by Kenny Delmar for "Allen's Alley," a part of Fred Allen's once-popular radio series..

And, finally, the last element in the series would star a somewhat dim-witted turtle, very slow on the uptake who, although only a boy, was already unhappy with his life and wanted to become something he was not, like a fast gunslinger in the Old West. His voice needed to be recognizable only in the sense that it would sound stupid, and he would be helped in his endeavors to change his life by Mr. Wizard the Lizard, whose voice should have the age and kindliness and accent of an old German professor. In every episode, Mr. Wizard would have to save the turtle from himself.

The turtle was originally named Toonerville, but copyright lawyers would eventually decree that because there had once been a daily newspaper comic strip titled *Toonerville Trolley*, the turtle's name should be changed. It was shortened to Tooter.

On Saturday morning, June 27, the day after Ingemar Johanson knocked out Floyd Patterson to win the Heavyweight Championship of the World, Buck and Chet met in the white Plymouth station wagon at the deserted gas station halfway between their homes to complete the pilot script and character summaries for *King Leonardo and His Short Subjects*.

By the time they parted, they were ready for a knockout of their own.

Nine

During the weeks that had been required to create the cartoon series, Buck had not been silent on the subject when he was with Gordon Johnson. Not on your life. It was very important that Gordon know his "request" was being acted upon, and acted upon just as quickly as possible. And so, one week after Chet had agreed to work on the series, Buck had reported to Gordon that he *thought* he had found the kind of creative group Gordon was looking for.

"Is it a group you'll be able to keep in line?" was Gordon's only question.

"Absolutely," Buck assured him.

"Good. Keep me up-to-date."

Ten days later, Buck had reported that he was now *sure* this was the right group. They had a hot property they were working on, and Buck believed Gordon was going to love it. The group, said Buck, was Total TeleVision productions.

The name "Total" had been chosen because it offered so many opportunities in terms of selling, and a few days later, still trying to keep Gordon's interest high, Buck had passed on to him a single sheet of paper which, Buck said, had been turned over to him by TTV. It read:

A NEW CARTOON SERIES
From Total TeleVision Productions
Total Concept: A new cartoon series with characters, voices, dialogue and
    action designed to appeal to all those who are young, whatever their
    age. Although the show follows the pattern of success laid down by

the best of other cartoon series, the characters and plots are new indeed, created by writers and artists who have extensive background in this field and know every phase of the business.

Total Entertainment: This is, in every sense of the word, a "total" package. Eight very unique characters, each with a well-developed personality; three completely different types of episodes; and eighteen minutes of new animation in every half-hour (only the titles and lead-ins and opens are repeated).

Total Flexibility: The elements of this show have been designed so that every program need can be readily fulfilled. The present format provides for a half-hour Saturday morning show, but this format can be revised to: increase or decrease the number of commercial positions, make the show ready for a nighttime slot, reduce the show from thirty to fifteen minutes, make the last episode of each show either complete in itself or a cliffhanger (continued until the next program).

Total TeleVision: That's what the above adds up to. And after you have had an opportunity to review the full show presentation, may we talk to you about the very reasonable *Total Price?*

"Sounds great," Gordon had said. What about the price they mention? Will it be about the same as Ward and Scott's?"

"It sure will. I checked on that right away."

"Good. I'm anxious to see what Total has in the way of a show."

Buck had been watching carefully to see how Gordon would react to the first part of this pitch, where it stressed the creative group's experience: "created by writers and artists who have extensive background in this field and know every phase of the business." Would Gordon ask for the details of this experience? Ask for names of other series these "writers and artists" had worked on? When he did not, Buck was more convinced than ever that Gordon knew the truth, knew that Buck, himself, was forming Total TeleVision productions.

This is why, when he entered Gordon's office the Monday afternoon following the completion of *King Leonardo,* Buck was so much at ease. He and Chet had created a knockout show, he was convinced, and Gordon was not going to ask any questions Buck would have difficulty answering. He felt sure of that.

This was a giant office, as it should have been for Gordon, both in terms of his size and his stature in the agency. There were many who felt Gordon would one day be president of DFS (and they were right). The office had four windows, maroon wall-to-wall carpeting and matching drapes, a very large mahogany desk, a large cabinet stocked with Metracal (the canned liquid diet of the day), two large leather armchairs and an oversized leather couch.

Smiling broadly, Buck said, "I heard from TTV this morning. They've still got some final retyping to do, but the material ought to be ready by the end of the week."

"Terrific," said Gordon, ripping off the bottom of a memo, folding it carefully and putting it into his mouth. "I want to see it as soon as they're ready."

"Absolutely."

"They can present right here," said Gordon, chewing paper enthusiastically. "Put the art right there on the couch and read me the script."

Buck nodded, but he was a little off-balance now. The word "art" had leaped out and struck him. "That's fine," he said, but he spoke a bit more slowly, more cautiously. "They aren't positive about the end of the week, but they're damn close."

"Good, good. I'm ready."

Buck left then, and he was not smiling. He walked quickly to his own office, a considerably smaller office next door to Gordon's, lifted the black phone on his desk without even sitting down, and dialed Chet's extension.

"We have to meet," said Buck.

"What's up?"

"Not now. Can you meet me after work?"

"Sure. But let's make it some place air-conditioned. It's hot as hell out there."

"How about the Rough Rider Room, 5:15?"

"I'll be there."

The Rough Rider Room was in the Roosevelt Hotel, only half a block from DFS. Buck arrived first, chose a small round table on the second gray-carpeted tier, and ordered a martini. There were few patrons this early.

Chet arrived right on time. He ordered his martini and then asked immediately, "What's up?"

"I told Gordon TTV was about ready to let him see the show."

"And?"

"He said 'great,' was really enthusiastic about it, and he suggested the show could be presented right there in his office."

Chet nodded, then shrugged. "So, what's the problem?"

Chet's drink arrived. They waited until the yellow-jacketed waiter had gone, then Buck said, "Gordon told me, 'They can put the art right there on the couch.'" Buck nodded and said again, "'put the art right there on the couch.'"

They were silent a moment, then Chet said, "It's a natural thing to say. He'd expect art. This is TV, not radio. He just has to be told that it's the next step."

Buck waved his hands back and forth. "I don't think so. He wants art now. He wants it first crack out of the box. I think that's what he was telling me, letting me know."

"Don't make too much out of it."

"I'm not. *He* did. It was the only thing Gordon asked for. 'They can put the art right there on the couch.' Why would he say that? I hadn't mentioned a damn thing about art and neither had he."

Chet took a swallow of his martini. "I'm telling you it's perfectly logical for him to expect art."

Buck shook his head. "It's more than that. He *wants* it. He's asking for it, telling me it has to be there in the first presentation."

Chet shrugged. "So okay, we have to go ahead and bring in a storyboard man."

Again, Buck waved his hands. "No, no. We haven't got time and it's too much of a gamble bringing somebody else in this early. We've got to have a front man to present to Gordon. That's bad enough. I don't want a fourth person before we get Gordon aboard."

"Then what do we do about the art?"

"All we need are character models. Just one pose for each of the eight characters."

"Maybe we could hire a freelance artist without getting into what it's for; just tell him exactly what we want for each of the characters."

"Too risky," said Buck. "Everybody in this business talks to damn near everybody else." He shook his head. "We can't take the gamble. We have to find another way."

Chet turned up his hands. "Like what?"

Buck smiled. "Like you."

Chet's eyes popped open like cue balls. "Are you crazy? I'm no storyboard artist."

"You're an artist; you're a painter. I've seen some of your work, and it's terrific."

"I'm glad you like it, but it doesn't make a damn bit of difference. What we need are cartoon models, the kind of stuff we can get from a good storyboard man. I don't do cartoons, understand? I paint."

Buck nodded, taking a swallow of his martini and emptying the glass. He ordered two more drinks, then said to Chet, "I've seen your doodles, I've seen your drawings, I've seen your paintings. You can do it. We have to get them fast and without letting anybody else in. You're our only hope."

Chet said nothing, glowering down into his empty martini glass.

Buck said, "We've got lots of pictures to help you." Almost from the beginning of the creative work, they had been collecting pictures, both live-action and cartoons, reflecting some of the characteristics they wanted in King Leonardo or Odie Colognie and the others. By now, they had quite a collection.

Still, Chet said nothing, his mouth a straight line.

Buck said, "If you don't do the models, I will."

Chet looked up quickly. You wouldn't!"

Buck nodded slowly. "Somebody has to do it."

Chet sighed audibly. "Okay, okay. I can't let all our great work go down the drain."

The martinis came then, and when the waiter had gone, Buck lifted his glass. "To *King Leonardo and His Short Subjects*."

Chet raised his glass. "I'll drink to that."

"And," said Buck, grinning ear to ear, "to our great new artwork."

Chet smiled in spite of himself and took a swallow of his martini.

Buck said, "I'll stall Gordon - get you until next week to finish the models."

"You're so kind."

"Meanwhile, I'll write the show's theme song and make a demo tape. We can't have my voice on it, so I'll try to get Andy Love to record it for us." Andy was a professional jingle singer and composer. Buck had worked with him many, many times.

"Good idea."

"And as long as we're here and our glasses are almost full, we ought to talk about the front man. We have to make the decision quickly…I want Tread."

Chet was surprised. "I thought you wanted Eli."

Eli Feldman was a good friend to both Buck and Chet, having worked with them for years at DFS before moving on to a better job with a better future at a TV company which produced commercials.

"I'd love to get Eli," said Buck, "but there's no chance. He's a partner in Pelican Films now, making good money with great prospects for more, and he has no desire to change his life."

"Did you ask him?"

"No, but I hinted around. There's just no reason for him to gamble, Chet. He likes his job, he likes the looks of his future, and he likes where he's living. Why the hell should he gamble?"

"Okay, so you want Tread. Why?"

Treadwell Covington was a longtime friend of Buck's and someone he had introduced to Chet a few years earlier. The three of them had enjoyed several lunches together. Buck asked, "Why not. He's a good guy."

"I've got no quarrel with that, but we're not talking good guy-bad guy. We're talking about whether somebody should be brought into the group because he can deliver. We know Eli can deliver. What about Tread?"

Buck said, "He's not happy with his job. The regional ad agency he works for doesn't pay enough, and Tread's future there doesn't look bright."

Chet shrugged. "That explains why he wants to make a change, but it doesn't say why he'd be good for us."

"There are a lot of reasons." Buck held up his right hand squeezed into a fist. He flipped up the fingers one at a time. "First, Tread's tall and has that prematurely gray hair and a North Carolina accent that sounds almost British. Perfect."

"Why?"

"That's exactly the kind of image that will impress Gordon. Believe me, I've seen it before…And number two…," he flipped up a second finger, "…Tread's done a helluva lot of recording work, which makes him the perfect guy to handle the recording of our soundtracks here in New York once we really get rolling. He's got the experience."

"So has Eli."

"We *can't* get Eli…And, third for Tread, he has no desire to leave New York the way we do. If we get TTV going, we'll need somebody here in the city, not just for the recording sessions, but for day-to-day business as well."

"He *likes* New York? A guy from Chapel Hill, North Carolina?"

"Seems to, maybe because his wife and daughters love it. Maybe because he's got a huge, gorgeous rent-controlled apartment on 72nd Street. It's a thing of beauty, and he pays peanuts for rent. I've already felt Tread out, without really saying what we're doing. He's anxious to get involved."

Chet turned up his hands. "Okay. If you're sure Gordon will be impressed, that's reason enough right there."

Buck smiled. "Tread will be terrific. I promise." (And Buck would be right. In producing TTV's soundtracks and in handling the day-to-day business in New York, Tread would do an excellent job.)

Chet said, "I just hope Gordon won't ask Tread who the writers and artists at TTV are."

"He won't. If he meant to do that, he would have done it long before now. Believe me, he knows what's happening here."

"Okay, then," said Chet, and he drained his martini glass. "I guess I'd better get the hell out of here and get started on the art."

Over the next eight days, as Chet slaved over the models, Buck had lunch with Tread Covington (who was quickly enrolled in the project, lending great enthusiasm), typed up and had copies made of all the pieces of the *King Leonardo* show including openings, closings, lead-ins, lead-outs and the format, as well as the Total TeleVision selling sheet Gordon had already seen, and put all this into booklets. He then sat down at the black piano in Hartsdale and wrote the theme for the show.

Envisioning a colorful parade of all the characters along the streets of Bongo Congo, Buck wrote:

> "Here comes Leonardo,
> Leonardo Lion,
> King of Bongo Congo,
> A hero lion or iron.
> Where Leonardo travels
> His subjects all go, too.
> There's Odie O. Colognie,
> The Fox and Hunter, too;
> Toonerville and Wizard,
> They're ready set to go.

So, everyone come join the fun
On King Leonardo's show!"

There would be a bridge and other verses (and, of course, the name Toonerville would be changed), but this was the basic (the original) theme.

"I like it," Chet said enthusiastically when he heard the demo. "It's catchy. But you didn't mention Biggy and Itchy."

Buck nodded, looking very serious. "That's one of the first rules about show themes. You aren't allowed to mention the chief villains."

"I didn't know that."

Buck grinned. "No wonder. I just made it up. Actually, there are other verses. Biggy and Itchy will be in there."

Three days later, thanks to longer days plus daylight saving time, Chet had ample light in which to unveil the models while he and Buck sat in the Plymouth wagon.

"My God!" said Buck, his eyes wide, "these are...these are dynamite!"

Chet had rendered each of the eight characters – King Leonardo, Odie, Itchy, Biggy, The Hunter, the Fox, Toonerville and the Wizard – on 14 x 17 boards, so that what they actually had in hand were eight magnificent paintings.

"Dynamite," said Buck, as he went over them again, placing some of them up on the dashboard. "All of them are great, but especially the King." He turned to Chet. "Does that guy look regal or what? He's a knockout...And Itchy. My God, he's a trip, isn't he?...And The Hunter, that magnificent blowhard. They're perfect, Chet. Absolutely perfect."

And so it was that just three days later, Tread Covington, arriving at DFS for his 9:30 A.M. appointment, was ushered into Gordon Johnson's office, shook hands with the world's only known paper chewer, and immediately began setting up the *King Leonardo* models on Gordon's oversized couch.

Showtime!

Ten

A few minutes before Tread arrived for his appointment with Gordon, Buck popped into Chet's office, uninvited and unannounced, and plopped down in the chair facing the desk.

"What are you doing here?" Chet asked suspiciously.

"Never mind. Just ignore me. I don't want to disturb you," he said with a smile. "I can see how busy you are, doodling all those pictures on the yellow pad."

Chet waved a finger. "Does that tone of voice imply that you think these doodles are unimportant? Too bad. I guess that's why you're an account man. You don't understand the creative process. Doodles like these stir the creative juices. This could be the beginning of a billion-dollar advertising campaign."

"Sure, sure," said Buck. "At least a billion."

"And what are *you* doing?"

"The truth?"

"The truth," said Chet.

"I'm hiding out. I don't want to be in my office when Tread gets to Gordon's office. It's too close to mine." He was slowly twisting one hand inside the other.

"Okay, but I thought we agreed not to talk *King Leonardo* business during office hours."

Buck nodded. "We did, we did. And it's a noble thought, so we won't do it. We'll sit here and act like nothing is happening. No meeting with Gordon which has our futures hanging in the balance. Nothing."

"So, what'll we talk about? It's going to be a little difficult just sitting here staring at each other."

"Twinkles."

"What?"

"We'll talk about Twinkles." This was a new brand of General Mills cereal for which Buck was responsible at the agency. It was a star-shaped cereal of oats and corn, with a cartoon pink elephant as its image ("Twinkles" was the name of the pink elephant) and, something no other cereal offered, there was a story booklet with a Twinkles adventure attached to the back of every box. The stories, new ones came out regularly, were written and drawn by Jerry Capp, brother of Al Capp who had created the comic strip, *L'il Abner*.

"Okay," said Chet, "we talk about Twinkles. But, please stop twisting your hands like you need soap and water. You're making me more nervous than I already am."

Buck put his hands in his lap. "Jack Mathis wants me to find an elephant like Twinkles and get him in Macy's Thanksgiving Day Parade." Mathis was in charge of Twinkles at General Mills.

Chet looked at his watch, then lit a cigarette. "He wants Twinkles in the parade. Why?"

"Free promotion. A ton of viewers will watch the parade on television, and we'd only have to pay the cost for the elephant."

"So, what's the problem?"

"The color."

Chet frowned. "I don't get you."

"Jack doesn't want just an ordinary-looking elephant. He wants one the same color as Twinkles on the packages: Pink. He wants me to have an elephant painted pink and march him in the parade."

Chet burst into laughter. "Painted pink!" Again, he laughed. "That's the craziest thing I ever heard of—quite a shock for all the drunks watching that parade. Is he serious?"

"Absolutely."

"Can you do it?"

"I don't know. But that's not my real problem. What worries me is: will a pink elephant in the Thanksgiving Day Parade make a positive statement for Twinkles, or will it anger millions of people?"

Chet knocked ashes from his cigarette. "Why would they get angry?"

"Because we'd have to paint the elephant pink, that's why. Is that any way to treat a dumb animal?"

"I don't know. They've got all kinds of paint these days. Or dye. Maybe vegetable dye. Maybe you can get some perfectly harmless pink dye."

"Even if I can, how would TV viewers know that? How would they know it was harmless?"

Chet shrugged. "I don't know. Put a sign on him. When he marches in the parade, have a sign that says, 'This pink paint is harmless.'"

"Oh, sure. And we could have another sign that—" He broke off as the phone rang, then said quickly, as Chet's secretary answered, "I told Tread to call me here after the meeting."

Chet looked at his watch nervously. "It's too soon, isn't it?" He rose and went to the door, listened a moment, then closed the door and came back to the desk. "It's for her."

Buck exhaled. He started to twist his hands together again, but then caught himself and dropped them into his lap. "This is damn near as bad as having a baby."

"Yeah. I think we're having labor pains. I wonder if Gordon—"

Buck interrupted by holding up his hands. "No, no," he said with forced dramatics. "No *King Leonardo* business, please. Back to Twinkles…The question comes down to this: Would having him march in the parade do more good than harm, or vice versa?"

"If it's that questionable, why not just drop the whole idea?"

Buck shook his head. "Perish the thought. You forget that this idea emanates from a client, and all clients are gods…to be obeyed whenever possible."

"Okay." Chet blew smoke into the air. "So you've got no choice."

"It's not that easy, my man. There's choice. But whatever I decide to do must be done only after much, much thinking, which must lead to absolute certainty that my decision is the right one. What do you think?"

"Well," said Chet, "I think the first thing you do is: A, you find out *if* you can get an elephant in the parade, and, B, if you can paint him pink. Why worry until you know it's possible." He ground out his cigarette in the green ashtray, stared down at his pad of doodles a moment and asked, "What if he hates it?"

"Mathis?"

Chet shook his head. "You know what I'm talking about. What if Gordon hates the show?"

"He won't."

"You don't know that. There are too many intangibles in this business. Maybe he hates jungles. Maybe he hates lions."

Buck shrugged. "Maybe he'll hate Tread."

"Maybe he'll hate the models."

"Or the story...or the music."

Chet nodded. "So what do we do if he hates it? Do we just give up? We worked our tails off creating this series..."

"Which just happens to be great."

"...which just happens to be great, and then maybe Gordon chews on his paper and destroys our show in one minute."

"I don't believe he'll do that."

"But, what if he does? What do we do, just give up?"

"Hell, no. We find out what it is that - "

Once again, the phone interrupted, and this time, after a few moments, Chet's secretary announced that the call was from Tread Covington. Chet used the desk phone, and Buck picked up the extension in front of the couch.

"He loved it!" Tread told them immediately. "He thought it was terrific."

"Hot damn!" Chet exploded.

"I knew it!" said Buck.

They spoke exuberantly for a few moments but then, not quite trusting the phones, they cut the conversation short.

The minute it was over, Buck said to Chet, "Let's go to lunch."

Looking at his watch, Chet laughed. "We can't go to lunch. It's not even eleven o'clock."

Buck stared at him as if lost in thought, then shrugged. "Okay, okay. I'll go back to my office."

"You know damn well Gordon will be looking for you."

Buck grinned and winked. "We did it, ol' buddy. We passed the acid test."

Chet nodded and grinned back. "Go hear what Gordon has to say. I'll meet you at the Teheran at 12:15."

Buck left, crossed the yellow linoleum-tiled open area and took the stairs to the seventh floor. He did not make it to his office. As he drew near, Gordon Johnson's secretary jerked her thumb toward her boss' office.

A tall, slender brunette in her early thirties, she had always been very kind and helpful to Buck. Now she said, "He's looking for you." She winked. "And he's anxious."

Buck turned into the corner office, paused just inside the doorway, then continued on as Gordon waved him in. "I saw the presentation from Total," he said immediately. "I like it. Just the kind of material I was hoping for."

"I'm glad," said Buck, sitting in the armchair facing the large desk. "I was pretty sure you'd like it."

Gordon tore off the bottom of a memo on his desk, folded it carefully until it was bite-sized, then popped it into his mouth and began chewing. "I want you to have them get this on storyboard right away."

"Got it," said Buck, nodding excitedly.

"The whole show. I told the Mills we'd present the full show."

Buck was surprised. "You've already called General Mills?"

Gordon smiled. "I called as soon as Tread left. I told Cy it was a hit series for sure. He wants us to bring the whole show to Minneapolis and give it a great presentation."

"Terrific."

"I want you to do the presenting, Buck, all of it – just like you presented the Twinkles material…and those *Rocky* episodes."

Buck nodded. "I'd love to do it."

"The music, too. That's a good tape. I like the parade idea."

"Right."

"When you have Total do the storyboard, be sure they make all the characters cartoony, the way King Leonardo is. That's the kind of stuff Gamma is used to inking and painting. We want to stick with that."

Again, Buck nodded. "Like King Leonardo. More anthropomorphic."

Gordon stopped chewing. "More what?"

"More like humans," Buck said quickly. "Less like an animal."

Gordon nodded slowly and began chewing again. "That's the ticket. More like humans, less like animals."

Buck took pen and pad from his inside coat pocket and made a note. "You want the complete show on boards," he said as he wrote, "and you want to be sure all the characters—the animals—are cartoony like the King."

"Right. How long do you think it will take to get that taken care of? I want to set the meeting with the Mills as soon as possible."

"I'm not sure, Gordy." Buck put his pen and pad away. "I'll check with Total and get back to you."

Nodding, Gordon took the paper from his mouth and tossed it into the wastebasket beside his desk. "The Mills is having another go-around with Jay, something about Boris Badenov insulting the FBI." He sighed. "Let's move this full speed, okay, Buck?"

"Full speed it is. You betcha." Buck rose and walked calmly to his office, closed the door and sat down behind the desk. Then the calmness fell away, as a broad grin captured his face. "Yesss!" he whispered aloud. "Yesss!"

Then he dialed home and gave the news to Grace.

Eleven

At an upstairs table in the Teheran Restaurant, their first martini in hand, Buck and Chet toasted their success with Gordon.

"We really did it!" said Buck.

"To King Leonardo!" said Chet.

They clinked glasses and took a swallow of their drinks.

Buck said, "Gordon's hot for us to move fast on this. He's anxious to set up the meeting with General Mills."

"It can't be too fast for me."

Buck looked down at the table. "I never told you—didn't want to dampen your enthusiasm—but I had a big worry about Gordon…which is why his being in a hurry to move ahead pleases me a lot."

Chet looked puzzled. "What kind of worry?"

Buck took a sip of his martini. "I was afraid that once he saw the script, he might figure that was enough."

"Enough for what?"

"Enough to keep Ward and Scott in line; use it as a kind of threat, but not go any further with the series."

Chet frowned. "That would have been a pretty rotten thing to do. We'd have wasted all that time and effort."

"Yeah." Buck winked. "But he didn't do it. He didn't do it all."

"So we have to move."

"Right. We've got to decide on a storyboard man." Buck had told Chet what Gordon had said about a complete storyboard and changes in some of the models.

Chet nodded. "I think Joe Harris is the man. I've worked with him a lot, and I promise you he's tops."

Joe Harris worked in the DFS TV art department.

Buck said, "I don't question Joe's ability to handle the job, you know that. I just don't like the idea of bringing a third member of DFS into Total TeleVision. And we don't have to do that."

"Who else could we get?"

"Eli Feldman's got a great guy who's not totally happy. Chris Ishi. He'd be terrific."

Chet nodded. "I know Chris, and you're right. He's great. But I've personally worked a helluva lot with Joe. I think that would give us a leg up."

"Maybe. But it would also make it a lot easier for us to find trouble. If what we're doing leaks out before we leave the agency, we could be up the creek."

"So, Joe will just have to be as careful as we've been…and as close-mouthed."

Buck did not respond.

Chet sighed loudly. "Look, we brought in Tread, your friend. So now, let's bring in Joe, my friend." He nodded. "Fair is fair."

Buck smiled slowly and then lifted his glass. "To friendship."

They touched glasses, and Buck asked, "Do you feel pretty sure Joe will want to come aboard?"

"He's crazy if he doesn't. We've damned near got a million-dollar contract already signed. You don't get many opportunities like that. I think he'll see it."

Chet was right. They met with Joe at the Rough Rider Room, and, after they provided some legal and personal answers to Joe's questions, he joined Total, going to work almost immediately. (And his contribution would prove invaluable to all Total TeleVision projects. He was, as Chet had said, quick, but much more than that he would prove able to capture on paper, with remarkable creativity, the characters Buck and Chet had in mind.)

Now, while Chet worked with Joe on the models, Buck completed theme songs for The Hunter and Toonerville (Tooter) Turtle, then had these put on tape by Andy Love's group. And Joe, with models in hand, went to work on a storyboard for the pilot show.

When all this was ready, Gordon and Buck took the complete package to General Mills in Minneapolis. Buck was nervous. Although he had pitched many commercials as well as Twinkles stories and even a few *Rocky* storyboards from Ward and Scott, never before had he been so personally involved in the work, nor had he ever felt, as he did now, that his future depended on the response to his effort.

Gordon delivered the business pitch perfectly, then Buck rose, hands sticky and tongue thick. It seemed as if almost everyone at the Mills was in that room. Buck set the scene, describing the kingdom of Bongo Congo, the King and his wise companion Odie, the King's beatnik brother and the infamous Biggy Rat. He played the theme song and then began acting out the scripts as he pointed to blow-ups of the board and did the voices and sound effects.

Smiles were there the minute this group heard the title, *King Leonardo and His Short Subjects*, and the laughter began soon after. The harder they laughed, the more into it Buck became. He began having great fun with the repeat lines he and Chet had given many of the characters, such as King Leonardo's, "That's the most *unheard* of thing I ever *heard* of," Itchy Brother's kooky, "Okay, Big. I dig," and The Hunter's laugh-provoking, "That a joke, son." The General Mills executives loved it all, and the moment the presentation was complete, they rose to their feet and gave *King Leonardo and His Short Subjects* a standing ovation.

No doubt about it now, the *King* had been sold. Oh sure, voice-actors had to be selected and a pilot half-hour produced and presented to the network before the deal was final and the contracts signed. But all of that, complex and time-consuming as it would be, was far more of a formality than the sale just made. At this point in TV history, the networks had such small budgets for kid programming, and yet were so anxious to improve their kid commercial sales, that any major advertiser who could offer a good kid show, virtually free of cost and partially sponsored, was almost assured of network agreement.

So they moved on to the auditioning and hiring of voice actors for the series - tremendous talents like Allen Swift, who supplied the voices for both Odie Colognie and Itchy Brother, and Jackson Beck, who did the same for King Leonardo and Biggy Rat. Buck and Chet had also expected to use one of these "imitators" to do the voice of The Hunter, but since this voice was to be very close to that of Senator Claghorn, Tread suggested that they try to get the original Claghorn, Kenny Delmar, who had created the character for Fred Allen's radio show. They did, and Delmar not only played The Hunter, he proved to be such a versatile voice, he became one of the voice-actors used by Total TeleVision most consistently during the coming years.

With the soundtrack complete, this along with the storyboard and theme music was turned over to PAT (Producers Associates of Television) for animation at Gamma. PAT (and later Leonardo Productions) would be the co-producer of all Total TeleVision shows sold to General Mills. Although Gordon Johnson was a major stockholder of PAT at that time, most of the corporation's day-to-day business would be handled by PAT's president, Peter Piech. Peter (who Buck always felt bore a striking resemblance to Peter Lorre) would be a tremendous help in keeping Total TeleVision shows on track, especially in terms of getting them completed on time at Gamma in Mexico.

While the *King Leonardo* pilot was in production, Buck and Chet turned their attention to a task requested by General Mills. Since Buck's presentation in Minneapolis, the only question the Mills had raised about *King Leonardo* had been a concern that the series idea might be limited in terms of plots. Beyond the pilot story with its *Prisoner of Zenda*-type plot, were there, General Mills wanted to know, enough additional plots to carry a long-term series?

Kenny Delmar, creator of Senator Claghorn, voice of The Hunter

Buck and Chet were certain the plots were there, but how could they put the question to rest in the minds of others? They found the answer in the creation of summaries for the first 26 two-part stories (52 episodes). Each of these summaries had five or six sentences explaining the plot. For example:

Episodes 4A and 4B *WAR ON THE CONGO* – Biggy and Itchy convince rival country Koko Loco that King Leonardo intends to make war to capture all the world's bongo drum business. Koko Loco prepares to attack first, and word reaches Bongo Congo by way of the bongo drummers. Odie has an idea. He uses a surprise "bongo attack" on the enemy troops, having all of King Leonardo's subjects playing a hot conga. Enemy troops are unable to resist. They throw down their guns and join the conga dancing chain.

Episodes 20A and 20B *GALLOPING GAMBLES* – Biggy and Itchy are taking over Bongo Congo by way of the underworld game. Biggy has imported hoodlums, and they are corrupting the kingdom, getting people to gamble on any kind of race. There are dog races and hog races, cat races and rat races, hare races and mare races. All the kingdom's earnings are going into Biggy's gambling syndicate. The country is falling apart. Families are starving. The King outlaws gambling, but to no avail. Odie steps in. He talks to all the dogs and hogs and cats and rats and hares and mares, gets them to fix the races so people win. Biggy and Itchy and their syndicate go broke.

Summaries like these did exactly what they were supposed to do. They relieved General Mills of any concern that there might be a shortage of plots. So they were a success. But down the road, as the Mills continued to demand these advance summaries for all TTV series, this weapon would backfire.

That, however, was far down the road. Right now, the pilot for *King Leonardo* was complete and NBC, the network for the show's Saturday morning debut in 1960, applauded the series and readied their 9:30 time slot for an October 15 kick-off.

And what a kick-off it was! No matter how high they might have set their sights, Buck and Chet could never have predicted the degree of success enjoyed by their first series.

"*King Leonardo* has the highest share of any children's program on television," Gordon Johnson wrote to Cy Plattes at General Mills on Dec. 1, 1960. "The *Leonardo* average audience ratings during the past two Nielsen reports have exceeded all other half-hour programs on daytime television!"

This ratings performance was all the more remarkable because *King Leonardo* had not been televised in the form originally expected. In order to make it easier for the Mills to "write off" the cost of this new cartoon material, old and inexpensive cartoons (*Heckle and Jeckle*) were included. Although cheap, they did not fit well with the *King Leonardo* material and had been televised many times. In spite of all this, *King Leonardo and His Short Subjects* were able to knock off the competition handily.

Shortly after Gordon Johnson's letter to General Mills, Chet found "personal reasons" for resigning from DFS and moving to Litchfield, Connecticut, and a few months later, Buck also found "personal reasons" for resigning and moving to Cape Cod, Massachusetts.

Very soon, thereafter, they were holding their Wednesday meetings at the 1812 House…which is exactly where this narrative left them on July 3, 1963, arguing about the impossibility of their latest assignment.

Twelve

"So, remember that," Buck was saying. "You were sure we didn't have a prayer of creating a cartoon series, but we sure as hell did, and we quit our jobs and got out of New York, and here we are." He held up his hands "Need I say more?"

They were deep into their second martini and, as often happened, they were the only patrons left in the 1812 dining room. Taking a swallow of his drink, Chet said, "That was a miracle and you know it. A frigging miracle. So that's it." He waved his hands back in front of him.

"That's what?"

"That's our miracle. We had it. One to a customer. Only a fool defies the odds more than once."

"Who said that?"

Chet grinned. "I did."

Buck laughed. "Okay, we'll do it your way." He became serious. "We'll just go back to Gordon and tell him we reject the challenge. We'll tell him we can't handle any direct competition with Ward and Scott. We don't want a chance at the NBC slot next year. In fact, we don't care whether we ever get another order or not. Thanks very much, but no thanks."

Chet shook his head. "That's not what I'm saying. We just...we just go to Gordon and explain our problem - ask for more guidelines, that's all."

"Oh, sure. Ward and Scott didn't get anything more in the way of guidelines, but we should."

"Because Ward has the General Mills contacts." He pointed at Buck. "Actually, we have the contacts too, only we don't dare get near them because of the way we started TTV."

"We have Gordon. He's our contact, and my guess is he knows as much as there is to know; as much as anyone knows. And he expects us to be able to win with the information we have right now." Buck drained his glass and held it up for the redhead to see. "Do you think Gordon wants us to lose this thing? Do you think he's against us?"

"No. I don't think he's against us *or* for us. But I don't believe he understands the creative process. Never has. So how would he know if we have enough information to go on?"

Buck shrugged. "Maybe he doesn't; maybe he's wrong. But do you really think we'd do ourselves a damn bit of good by asking him for more help? I think it would just make him disappointed in us. And, anyhow, I don't think he's got more help to give."

"Because he's told us all he knows about the contest?"

"Or all that he thinks is important. We have to take what we've got and look at it in a different way; focus on that information. You say we need guidelines. Okay. Let's make what we know into guidelines, enlarge on what we have."

The redheaded waitress arrived with their third drinks. "Thanks, sweetheart," said Chet. "You can bring our shrimp anytime you're ready."

"Right away," she said.

When she had gone, Chet asked Buck, "When you say focus on what we've got, you mean, 'no frogs,' right? It's not a helluva lot."

"'Stay away from frogs.' Those were Gordon's words. 'Stay away from frogs.' And before that, he said that our show concept had to be better than anything on TV."

Chet frowned. "You never mentioned he said that – 'better than anything on TV'."

Buck waved his hands back and forth. "You're right. Scratch that. It's not what he said. That's me editorializing. Gordon never said it." Buck stopped, then nodded to himself as he thought back to the Gamecock meeting.

"So, what *did* he say?" Chet asked impatiently.

"He said the series had to be great." Immediately, Buck shook his head. "No, no. He didn't say great. The word he used was 'super.' And he said it twice. 'All I can tell you,' he said, 'is that you've got to have a super series.' Then added, 'And I mean *super*."

Chet took a swallow of martini, then toyed with Gordon's word. "Super."

"That's the word." Buck nodded and winked. "Let's focus on it. It's all we've got."

There was a moment of silence and then, looking directly at each other, they shouted in unison, "A superhero! A superhero!"

The redhead hurried to their table. "Is everything all right?"

They laughed, and Chet said, "Everything is perfect."

"Absolutely," said Buck. "Sorry about the noise."

"That's okay," she said, smiling. "I'll bring your shrimp right over."

The moment she had gone, Chet said excitedly, "If Gordon wants a 'super' series, we'll give him a 'super' series."

"What could be more super than a superhero?"

Now Chet lifted his glass and Buck did the same. "To our first superhero," said Chet. They touched glasses and took a swallow of their drinks.

"Why the hell didn't we get this idea before?"

Chet shook his head. "Who knows, but I can feel it's right. We've turned the corner."

"Do you know something? When I was a kid, I was one of the biggest Batman fans you could ever imagine. He was my favorite hero."

"He was a good one."

Buck said, "There are a lot of superheroes, but mostly in comic books, I think. Not on TV."

"I liked Captain Marvel, myself. Shazam!"

"That's what Gomer Pyle says. 'Shazam.'"

"Who's Gomer Pyle?" Chet asked.

Buck laughed. "He's the newest character on Andy Griffith's show, supposed to be a country bumpkin who still reads comic books, and whenever he gets excited, he says, 'Shazam!' He's funny."

"That's what we're going to be, right?"

"What?"

"Funny. We're going to make our show funny."

"Absolutely," Buck agreed. "Otherwise, how could we have fun writing the show?"

"We couldn't."

Buck nodded. "So we want a superhero series that's got comedy. Now all we have to do is figure out what it is."

Chet snapped his fingers. "Do you know what comes to me?"

"What?"

"A TV show I saw a couple of weeks ago. A *Lucy* rerun."

Buck was surprised. "You? Watching *Lucy* reruns? What happened to the Educational Channel?"

"Evan was watching. I wanted to share the experience with my son."

Buck nodded. "Understandable. I won't tell anybody you were watching normal television."

"I'm glad I did. Have you ever seen a *Lucy* episode about Superman?"

"Not that I remember."

"Funny. And clever. I laughed like hell, and so did Evan. Lucy was giving this big birthday party for her kid – Little Ricky – and she was competing with all the other mothers of Ricky's friends to have the best birthday party of all. So she talked Big Ricky into inviting Superman to the birthday party."

Buck chuckled. "I can feel the ending coming already."

"Lucy didn't wait for Superman's answer, of course. She went ahead and told everybody he was coming - bragged about it to the other mothers."

"And then he couldn't make it."

Chet nodded. "Guess who decided she had to pretend she was Superman?"

"Lucy."

"She put on this crazy costume and went out on the ledge to make an entrance through the window. But what do you know? The real Superman showed up, which would have been great, except that the window slammed shut and Lucy got stuck out on the ledge, pigeons crapped on her, and it started to rain. Luckily, Superman came to the rescue."

"That's funny," said Buck.

"What made it so great was the way they played it: Straight as an arrow. They took it all very seriously. And that's what made it so damn funny."

"Lucille Ball always does that with her shows. They have excellent comedy because the actors play it like it's drama." He stopped a minute, then pointed at Chet. "That reminds me of something. Did I tell you about my plane ride with Ray Goulding? He's half the Bob and Ray team."

"I know that. I wrote a series of commercials for Bob and Ray a few years ago." He shook his head. "You didn't tell me about seeing him."

"I guess Gordon's assignment pushed it out of my mind."

Before he could go on with the story, their waitress arrived with the double shrimp cocktails. When she had gone, they busied themselves for a moment adding horse radish to the cocktail sauce, then spooned it onto their plates.

"So what happened with Ray Goulding?" Chet asked.

"He took the same plane I did from Hyannis to LaGuardia, and during the entire flight, he was laughing like hell, laughing at something he was reading. After he left the plane, I got a chance to find out what he'd been reading. He left it behind."

When he went no further, Chet said, "Okay, I'll bite. What was it?"

"A newspaper. The *Boston Globe*. Just a normal issue of the *Boston Globe*. I went through it page by page, and unless you count the comics or maybe the way the Boston Red Sox play baseball, there wasn't a single bit of humor in the entire paper."

Chet shrugged. "So, what was he laughing at?"

"At the news, believe it or not. All the news items. Only I think he moves the stories a little to one side or the other, a little off-center. And it makes them damn funny. My guess is that's what he and Bob do when they write their routines. They take perfectly normal stuff and keep the basic facts the same, but they add or subtract a little something. You know what I mean?"

"Sure. That's exactly the way I wrote those commercials for them—a little off-center."

Buck nodded. "They seem to be playing it straight, but the slight change they make keeps it funny. That's why Goulding was laughing on the plane."

"Which is pretty much the same kind of thing I saw on the *Lucy* episode."

"Absolutely. And with the right storyline, this could be the perfect way to appeal to a broad age-bracket on TV. The younger kids will get a kick out of the straight story—the adventure—while the older kids go for the off-center humor."

"But no laugh-track."

"No, no," said Buck. "That would kill it for the younger kids. It's got to be played straight as an arrow."

Chet dipped a shrimp in sauce and took a bite. "So what's the next step?"

"We've made a helluva lot of progress. We know a lot about the kind of show we want, and we know we want a superhero at the center."

"Is he human or animal?"

"We ought to stick with making the central characters animals. It's worked up to now. Why change?"

"Especially since Ward is using a frog."

"Right," said Buck. "We ought to figure the hero will be something other than human, but I don't think the kind of non-human is the most important question now. What we need next is to consider the kinds of superheroes already out there—the ones we don't want to use."

"And that might lead us to the kind of character we *do* want." He nodded. "Okay, we've got our work cut out for us, but at least now I do think we've got a prayer. We're on the verge of another miracle." He pulled a yellow pad closer and took his pen from his pocket. "Let's make some notes."

Buck reached down and picked up his briefcase, pulled out a folder and then returned the briefcase to the floor. "I've got my research on kid shows."

"So, what do we want to avoid?"

After reading a moment, Buck said, "There are a lot of superheroes in comic books, but only a couple on TV." He was thumbing through the folder as he talked. "The guys I remember from the 1940s—Superman, Batman, Captain Marvel—none of them have had a cartoon series on TV, and only Superman has made it at all."

Chet nodded. "George Reeves' serial. He was the one in that *Lucy* episode. He died, didn't he? Got shot?"

Buck shook his head. "He shot himself—four years ago. There was a lot of mystery. Nobody knows why he did it. He was okay financially, but for some reason he shot himself, and it didn't look like an accident."

They were silent a moment, then Chet said, "So, I guess he wasn't bulletproof after all."

They laughed.

Buck said, "That series was in production for seven years, 1951 to 1957. And it's still in syndication. It started out in prime-time, then the reruns moved to late afternoon. Now, it even turns up on Saturday morning."

"How are the ratings?"

"Not great, but it's been run to death. And it's black-and-white."

"What else have you got?"

"Well, Superman never made it into cartoon form, but an imitation of him did."

"Who was that?"

"Our current competition, for *King Leonardo*."

"Mighty Mouse?"

"That's it. Originally, the character was called 'Supermouse.' Of course, he didn't start out on TV. This was a theatrical cartoon first."

"I've seen a few episodes to check out the competition. There's nothing funny about that show. It's just straight adventures."

"That's right, but it wasn't originally supposed to be that way. It was supposed to be a parody, but that never happened. A guy named Klein...," Buck looked up from the folder, "...I don't have his first name. Anyhow, he was a writer at Terrytoons, and when Superman popped up in D.C. Comics, he thought it would be great to do something like that as a theatrical cartoon parody. His idea was to make the lead character a fly – Superfly."

"What happened?"

"Paul Terry, the head of the studio, liked the idea of a Superman rip-off, but not as a parody. He wanted adventure. He changed the creature to a mouse, and had no comedy overtones at all."

"When was that?"

Buck looked down at the folder. "1942. They made the first four cartoons as *Supermouse*, then changed the name to *Mighty Mouse*."

"When did it get to TV?"

"1955. CBS put on *The Mighty Mouse Playhouse*, using the theatrical cartoons with a live host. Later, made-for-TV cartoons were added."

"But it's all adventure. No comedy."

Buck nodded. "Just like the episodes you watched – Superman for mice. I don't like the show at all, but don't knock it. *King Leonardo* was kicking the hell out of CBS when the competition was *Captain Kangaroo*. But when they replaced the *Captain* with *Mighty Mouse*, our ratings got hurt. I think that means even a bad superhero can rate damned well."

Buck put down the research folder, and they concentrated on their food and drink. Buck said, "Some of the *Mighty Mouse* episodes I've seen are music from top to bottom, like miniature operas."

"Operas?"

"Yeah. The *Mighty Mouse* theme is like that, too."

"Opera. That sounds kind of funny."

"I know, but it doesn't play like that. There's no humor in anything the mice do, no matter what your age. There's nothing to produce laughs.

We need to find a way to change that – move it off-center – if we're going to have a superhero who brings a little humor."

Chet lifted his glass, but stopped abruptly before it reached his mouth. "In that *Lucy* episode I told you about, they had something we might be able to use. Lucy was talking to her best friend..."

"Ethel."

"...yeah. They were wondering how Superman should make his entrance at the birthday party. Lucy said that Superman usually came in by crashing through a wall."

Buck laughed.

Chet said, "But Ethel told Lucy her husband wouldn't like that."

"Fred."

"Yeah. Fred wouldn't like Superman crashing through the wall, so they'd have to find some other way for him to come in."

"That's terrific," Buck said excitedly, catching the idea immediately. "You always see Superman crashing into places in his comic strip or comic books, and nothing bad ever happens. And it's the same with George Reeves' show." He laughed again. "But not with ours. We'll have pieces of the ceiling almost knocking people out."

"Or pieces of the wall. Or the windows. And think of the stuff we can do with our hero in the sky if his attention happens to be diverted. He bumps into airplanes or tall buildings."

"Chimneys or billboards."

"Radio stations and TV antennas."

Chet was nodding rapidly. "And what about bullets? When they bounce off our superhero, they barely miss hitting people nearby."

"People are ducking all over the place."

They were laughing hard now.

"That's funny as hell," said Buck. "Exactly the kind of stuff we need."

"We'll be playing it straight, because that's really what would happen, only it's always carefully avoided by Superman and Mighty Mouse."

They laughed some more. Chet took his last bite of shrimp, and raised his hand for the redhead. "What other superheroes are on TV?"

Buck lifted the folder from the table and looked at it a moment. "There's just one other, and I'm not sure he ought to be classified as a superhero."

"Why not?"

"I'm talking about Courageous Cat."

Chet shook his head. "Don't know him."

The waitress arrived then, and Chet ordered their coffee.

"Dessert?" she asked.

Chet smiled. "You know we never have dessert."

She smiled back, showing beautiful white teeth. "There's always a first time." she removed their plates and glasses.

As she left, Buck looked at his research folder again. "Courageous Cat has been around for a couple of years. One source says 1960, but that's wrong. The series didn't get on TV until 1961. It was syndicated."

Chet turned up his hands. "So is it a superhero show or not?"

"Depends on your interpretation. Is Batman a superhero?"

"Sure. You called him one yourself."

"But he doesn't have any superpowers. He's just a normal, muscular person with a whole bunch of expensive gadgets."

"Some gadgets. They let him do just about anything he wants to. I say he's a superhero."

"Okay, then so is Courageous Cat. Guess who created him?"

"Jay Ward."

"No, no. I've already given you a hint."

"Please," said Chet sarcastically, "I'm not good at quiz games, and the suspense is killing me. Who created Courageous Cat?"

The answer had to wait. The waitress arrived with their coffee and check. It was a unique check. Room rent was on it as well as martinis and shrimp and coffee. They thanked the redhead and told her they would see her next Wednesday.

"Have a good week," she said as she left.

Putting cream and sugar in his coffee, Buck said, "Okay, here it comes. The creator of Courageous Cat was…Bob Kane!"

"My God," said Chet, with mock amazement. "Bob Kane…who the *hell* is Bob Kane?"

Buck smiled and took a swallow of coffee. "He just happens to be the man who created my favorite comic book hero, Batman. And—surprise, surprise—Courageous Cat is a cartoon rip-off of Batman. The cat has a partner, Minute Mouse, who is an animal version of Robin; they work their wonders in Empire City—remember Gotham City in *Batman*?; they live in the Cat Cave, not to be confused with the Bat Cave; and they drive around in a Catmobile."

"Is it funny? It sounds funny."

Buck shook his head. "That's the peculiar part. It isn't funny at all. Strictly adventure, and pretty kid-ish adventure at that. The only thing even remotely funny about it are the gadgets the heroes and villains come up with. It's not much of a series, if you ask me. The scripts aren't much, the animation is so slow and stiff it looks starched, and the characters are as dull as dishwater."

"Is that good or bad?"

"What do you mean?"

"You're telling me that kid TV has only two superhero series; one we've both seen and don't care for, *Mighty Mouse*—we'd go crazy writing that kind of stuff—and the other one, *Courageous Cat*, which you say is stiff and dull. So, why the hell should we be trying to come up with a superhero series?"

Buck winked. "First, because Gordon told us General Mills wants a "super" series, and we've decided to make that mean 'superhero'; second, the fact that the only two superheroes series on the air are stiff and dull without any laughs only proves the field is wide open; and third, deciding to make our new assignment a superhero series means we're no longer operating with a map of the world." He grinned. "I think we're digging in gold country. I can feel it."

"Okay, okay," said Chet, picking up the enthusiasm. "I'm with you."

They finished their coffee and paid the check, packed all the gear into their briefcases, and went out to their cars, side by side in the parking area.

They stopped at the cars and Buck, always feeling it was his responsibility to mete out the "assignments," said, "We've done a helluva lot today. To keep moving it along, let's each of us come up with ten names or titles – names for the superhero or titles for the show, either one. Maybe this can help lead us to the show, itself."

"Okay," said Chet. "That sounds good. Ten names or titles."

They climbed into their cars. Buck was parked nearest Route 9, so he backed out first, and turned the little Renault toward the road. Suddenly, he was shocked by loud "explosions" at the back of the car. Assuming the Renault was in trouble, he stopped quickly, but when he turned around, he saw that the noise was due to Chet, banging on the car.

Chet hurried to the driver's window.

Opening the window, Buck asked, "What's wrong?" He was sure Chet wanted to tell him about some kind of problem with the car.

"Our superhero," said Chet excitedly. "We ought to do the same thing for him we did for Tennessee."

Buck's thoughts were still caught up in concern for his Renault. "What the hell are you talking about?"

"Let's find our superhero the same way we found the hero for our educational series. That could give us the whole ball of wax."

Buck's eyes widened as the idea sunk in. "Sure," he said. "Sure. Find our superhero just the way we found Tennessee. That could do it!"

They were talking about the hero of *Tennessee Tuxedo and His Tales*, a new cartoon series which had not made its debut (this would happen more than two months later on Sept. 28, 1963), but already they considered it a tremendous success in many ways. And not without reason.

Thirteen

The meeting that spawned the groundbreaking *Tennessee Tuxedo* took place in October of 1961, and it was a meeting that very nearly did not take place at all. Buck and Chet were going into New York for a totally different reason. As always, they felt it would be wise to phone Gordon Johnson, let him know they would be there in case he wanted to take time to see them, whether for business or pleasure or a combination of both.

When Buck called, Gordon's answer at first was no. Clearly, he was up to his ears in client business, did not have anything that needed immediate discussion and did not have time for socializing. But then, after he had asked for a rain check, Gordon suddenly changed his mind. "Wait a minute," he said, barely catching Buck before the connection was broken. "Maybe there is something. You might not be interested, but what the hell. Let's have lunch."

So they arranged to meet at the Gamecock at 12:30. In the hours before that appointment, Buck and Chet, having arrived in the city very early, would have a meeting about an entirely different kind of show, a series titled *Parrot Playhouse*.

Soon after they left DFS and moved out of New York, their livelihood now depending on the success of Total TeleVision productions, Buck and Chet realized they could not simply continue writing scripts for *King Leonardo* and hoping that General Mills might ask them to create additional TV series. They knew that the *King Leonardo* orders would last only until the Mills had accumulated four years of TV shows (General Mills felt that the key age group who bought most of their cereals covered a four-year span). Once this number of shows had been purchased for a particular series, orders would end. So if sales were to continue with General Mills, other series would have to be sold by TTV. And since that was iffy, Buck and Chet decided TTV had better light some fires in other areas if they hoped to stay in business.

Toward this end, they decided to strike out in a new direction, live-action rather than animation. Obviously, they would keep this avenue (animation) open for Gamma and General Mills, but in terms of broadening their sales base, live-action seemed a logical choice. They would still be creating for children, but live actors would be used. Real people.

The most immediate problem was that live actors had never been able to beat a good cartoon series in the ratings. Why? In terms of kid actors, which Buck and Chet wanted to use, the reason seemed to be twofold. First, because the adventures of the kid actors in shows like *Our Gang* were so trivial, they tended to be boring for TV kids used to a lot of action. Second, the dialogue of the kids was so disappointing in terms of "acting," that it never quite came off.

Out of this came the creation of a live-action concept titled *Parrot Playhouse*, to be a Saturday morning kid show. All the actors would be kids, appearing in ten-minute parodies of popular prime-time programs, past and present: *I Love Lucy, This is Your Life, Gunsmoke, The Honeymooners,* and on and on. There would be two ten-minute parodies per half-hour, putting a *Gunsmoke* with a *This Is Your Life*, for example.

The kicker—the gimmick which would make the dialogue truly come to life—was the fact that all the kid voices would be removed and adult voices dubbed in with perfect lip sync. Buck and Chet were convinced the series would be extremely funny with plenty of action, and to prove their point they shot a three-minute 8-millimeter sound film with Buck's Fairchild camera and tried it out on a schoolroom full of kids. They went wild.

Needing a production company, Buck and Chet worked out a joint-venture with one of their oldest and most trusted friends, Eli Feldman and his company, Pelican Films. As virtually 50/50 partners, TTV and Pelican would own the new *Parrot Playhouse*. It was in order to sign this agreement that Buck and Chet went to Manhattan on Monday, October 16, 1961. In a morning meeting at Pelican, the contract for *Parrot Playhouse* was reviewed in detail and signed. Then after considerable discussion, it was decided that the first program to be parodied would be *Gunsmoke*. Buck and Chet promised to deliver a ten-minute script in two weeks.

Now it was time to move on to their 12:30 lunch at the Gamecock.

"You may not be interested at all," Gordon told them in the "meeting room," after they had reminisced a bit and enjoyed a couple of swallows of their martinis. "I've already tried this on Jay Ward, and he gave me a flat-out no. I won't blame you if your answer is the same."

Although he did not have a clue about what Gordon had in mind, Buck said, "We want more orders, Gordy. TTV is interested in any new opportunity you have." (Buck and Chet could speak more openly now, with Gordon or anyone else, about the needs and desires of TTV because—surprise, surprise—they had been asked to join Total TeleVision productions, and were now "part of the company.")

Gordon said, "The Mills is interested in something educational." He smiled. "That turned off Jay completely. What about you?"

Buck and Chet looked at each other and smiled. They had already been talking about coming up with an educational series. Chet was especially interested in creating such a property. Now he said, "We're interested. Very interested. What's it all about?"

"Newton Minot," said Gordon. "General Mills would like to demonstrate that they've paid attention to Minot's comments about kid television. So, they'd like to see a presentation on a five- or six-minute educational segment—an inner series—they could use in some of their shows."

Chet asked, "Why just an inner segment? Why not come up with a new concept that would support a complete half-hour series?"

Gordon shook his head. "Because it won't rate. Even if the Mills buys the segment you come up with—which I ought to warn you is doubtful—they'll expect the rest of the show to carry that segment. They know kids won't tune into education."

"Maybe they will," said Buck, "if they have the right show to choose, one that *entertains* while it educates."

"*And* gets high ratings?" Gordon answered his own question by shaking his head. "It can't be done. And whereas the Mills would like to demonstrate that they've made a real effort to do what Minot wants, they're not going to do it if it means low ratings. Even if the Mills wanted to, the networks wouldn't go along."

Buck said, "I read somewhere that the networks are ready to devote some airtime to Minot's cause."

Five months earlier in a speech where FCC Chairman Newton Minot had called television "a vast wasteland," he had insisted that Nielsen ratings should not be influential in the choice of programming for children, and a few months later (September 1961) Minot stated that the majority of TV programming for children was "dull, grey and insipid." He also talked about lighting a few million candles to bring "our children out of the darkness."

As Buck had just suggested, the networks' response to Minot had been to promise they would devote "some airtime" to educational programming.

Now, Gordon said, "They'll have to do something—a weekday half-hour or on the weekend—but the ratings will be a test pattern. They'll just do it for brownie points, so the FCC won't come down on them."

(Each of the networks would do this in 1962. The shows would be *Exploring* on NBC, *Reading Room* on CBS, and *Discovery* on ABC. None of these programs would ever capture a success-sized audience.)

Chet said, "We think it's possible to create a series that will win its time period and yet educate the kids."

"Great," said Gordon skeptically. "What is it?" He took a swallow of his martini.

"We just started noodling the idea," said Buck.

"But we can do it," said Chet confidently. "A complete half-hour."

Buck nodded. "We're convinced of that."

Gordon smiled indulgently. "Okay, okay. But I might point out that it's never been done in the history of television…or radio, for that matter."

"So, we'll be the first," said Buck.

Laughing, Gordon said, "Sounds good to me. But let's not worry right now about whether it turns out to be a segment or a complete show, because, whatever it is, you'll have big trouble selling it."

"Why?" asked Chet. "You said the Mills wants one."

"Mostly," said Gordon, "I think they want somebody to go through the motions. They want to be able to show the do-gooders that they gave it a serious try. Oh, I think Cy would be happy if it could be done, but most of the others, they don't really care."

"We can do it," Buck said again.

"Okay," said Gordon, "if you want to take a crack at it, go ahead. We might even do a pilot. But I'm being straight with you. Even if you're absolutely sure you've come up with the perfect concept, you're going to have one helluva job convincing the Mills." He grinned. "Hell, you're going to have a helluva job even convincing *me*."

So this was the challenge. But first there was a script to write for *Parrot Playhouse* (as well as the regular weekly scripts for *King Leonardo*). The *Gunsmoke* parody, which would eventually be titled "Spoofs 'n Saddles," offered a ton of funny Western clichés with lookalike kid actors in the roles of Marshal Matt Dillon, Kitty Russell, Doc Adams, the limping deputy Chester B. Goode, as well as a fast-gun villain (who would end up being about three feet tall). The script was sent to Pelican right on schedule, and they began casting for the film which would be shot in a Western "town" located in New Jersey.

With the *Parrot* script completed, Buck and Chet could turn their attention to Gordon's educational project, but they would quickly discover that finding out how to entertain and educate simultaneously (and gain high ratings) would be their toughest challenge to date. Oh, they had sounded very sure of themselves when they spoke with Gordon, but at the time they had actually given educational television only a superficial examination. It seemed logical to them that they should be able to create an educational series which would rate successfully, but they had not made an attempt to do this. Now they did, and there were no ready answers.

In the beginning, whatever they brought forward as an educational idea soon seemed to be a turnoff in terms of entertainment. They had ideas about numbers, for example, ideas they felt were fun and entertaining. Did you know that any number when added to nine always returns to itself? Consider the number 2. Add it to nine and it becomes 11, a very different number it seems. Yet, if you add together the two digits of 11—1 and 1—they add up to two, the original number. Or add nine to six, and the product is 15, quite a different number. But if you add one and five, you get what? Six, of course, the original number.

They felt that numbers used like this could become characters, and their interaction could become stories; adding, subtracting, multiplying, dividing could be turned into plots that would entertain *and* excite children's interest in education. Buck and Chet had collected such "interaction" in many fields—sociology, physics, history, geography, zoology.

They considered working in this kind of material a little at a time, sprinkling it throughout episodes like seasoning on a salad, creating a typical adventure series and then letting bits of education pop up like mushrooms as the hero or heroes moved about the world. But each time they tried this, the moment the look of education appeared on the screen, they worried that the kids might be gone.

What they desperately needed was something to lock the kids to the TV set. What could this be? What could be done to make kids want to watch education? What could be done to make kids want to stay tuned to a particular show when the screen began offering education?

The answer was that the education had to be *transformed*, turned into something the kids wanted or needed, turned into something they wanted or needed *desperately*. But what? What could this transformation make out of education?

They found the beginning of their answer by returning to one of the most basic of all storylines: Get the hero up a tree, let the villain throw rocks at him, then let the hero *find something* that enables him to get down from the tree and defeat the villain. One of the best-known cartoon series based on this formula was *Popeye*. Let Bluto get Popeye up a tree and throw rocks at him, then let Popeye get hold of some spinach and, with his newfound strength, let him get down from the tree and defeat Bluto.

That was the answer. Education had to be transformed into "spinach." The hero had to need a can of education, just like Popeye needed a can of spinach, in order to save the day. The education would arm the needy hero—give him "strength"—and he would conquer the villains.

Finally, they knew how to transform education. Now, all they needed was a series.

Fourteen

Although they were certain now that they knew how to transform education so that kid viewers would actually *want* it, Buck and Chet did not have the program concept in which this transformation could be used. And it did not come easily. Many storylines were discussed and discarded.

Thanksgiving came and went, and by the time the Christmas holidays rolled around, all Buck and Chet had on paper was a very skeletal plot which could use the "can of spinach" technique: Two kids in need of knowledge (why?) get help from an absent-minded magician who can, in order to help the kids learn, turn them into anyone or anything—animal, vegetable or mineral—and take them forward or backward in time.

This was barely a start, for it offered no meaningful character for the kids and no meaningful reason for their need of knowledge.

Meanwhile, the "Spoofs 'n Saddles" pilot of *Parrot Playhouse* had been completed, not just the filming, but also the substitution of adult voices for those of the kid actors.

Unfortunately, the lip-syncing was not as on-the-mark as Buck and Chet had hoped it would be, but Eli assured them that enough had been learned with this pilot so that future episodes would be remarkably improved. "With some of the techniques we've worked out," he said, "you'll think those kids were *born* with adult voices."

Normally, the next step would have been to set up presentation appointments with each of the heads of kids programming at the three networks, but Buck and Chet were so enthusiastic about the uniqueness of this kid-actor concept that they wanted to try and take it right to the top. Toward this end, they turned to Stuart Upson, probably the brightest light ever to shine at DFS, a former boss of both Buck and Chet and a good friend. He also happened to be a friend and neighbor of Tom Moore, the president of ABC.

Stu was kind enough to help Buck and Chet set up an early January meeting with Moore. On that date, Eli and Buck and Chet arrived at ABC promptly with their ten-minute pilot and an impressive printed pitch for the *Parrot Playhouse* concept. The presentation took place in the ABC Theater—red walls and carpet, red seats, even a red curtain for the movie screen.

They sat in the balcony, looking down at a large stage. Tom Moore, a burly moon-faced man, arrived with two tightly-suited associates who treated Eli and Buck and Chet like lepers while treating Tom Moore like a movie mafia boss, leaping up to light his cigarette or turn down his theater seat or, later, opening the door for him.

Moore himself, quite affable, said, "Stu Upson tells me you've got something I ought to see."

"We sure have," said Buck enthusiastically. "This is not like any kid show ever produced before. We promise you that."

The presentation booklets were given to the three members of ABC, and Eli, Buck and Chet quickly explained the concept and mentioned some of the shows which would be parodied: sitcoms, game shows, private-eyes, westerns, whatever found favor in prime-time. With the pitch complete, the moment of truth had arrived. The projectionist was signaled to roll the film, and everyone turned to face the screen as the curtain opened.

In presenting a comedy pilot, this is always a difficult moment for those doing the selling, especially when, as in this case, there is no laugh-track. The sellers cannot laugh too quickly or too often or too loudly at their own product for fear of producing a negative effect. On the other hand, they cannot afford to sit there like a stone if they have something which is supposed to be funny.

The film began, and the initial scenes—shots establishing the story—offered only two or three lightweight wordplay gags. Eli and Buck and Chet chuckled carefully, but Moore did not, and his two henchmen sat like frigid mannequins, cold as the weather outside. But then, as the two-gun villain was introduced, a tiny blond boy dressed all in black, Tom Moore abruptly laughed, a booming laugh that quickly defrosted his flunkies. And when Moore laughed again, this time at the tiny villain's deep bass voice, the flunkies were only a split-second behind him. From that point on, as Moore's booming laugh continued throughout the pilot, his associates tried to outdo each other as to which one could laugh the loudest.

When the lights came on, Moore said immediately that he thought *Parrot Playhouse* was a "spectacular idea. Funny as hell." And he asked about costs and time needed for delivery, also about how the two ten-minute parodies be held together. Then he promised to respond quickly, and asked that no one else be shown the film until his office had been heard from. He was assured that this would be the case. As Eli and Buck and Chet departed, it seemed that their leprosy had undergone a miraculous cure. Moore's two assistants fell over each other trying to press the flesh.

This was without a doubt the single most successful presentation ever in the lives of Eli and Buck and Chet, so successful that the three of them went immediately to Central Park's Tavern on the Green Restaurant where they enjoyed one of the longest lunches on record, constantly punctuating the meal with martini toasts to the success of *Parrot Playhouse*, and with bursts of laughter at the lunacy of Tom Moore's "associates."

Is success contagious? It always seemed that way to Buck and Chet. If events began going well in one area, then, invariably, events would soon be doing the same in other areas. And that is exactly how it was with their educational assignment. Only three days after that great ABC Theater meeting with Tom Moore, Buck and Chet happened to see on TV a 36-year-old stand-up comic named Don Adams. They saw him Wednesday night on *The Kraft Music Hall*, hosted by Perry Como, and then remembered seeing him once before on a late-night program, probably Steve Allen's *Tonight!* show, doing a routine about modernistic art.

What knocked them out about Don Adams was that he had both the looks and the voice of a cartoon character, exactly the kind of "hero" they could use. He had the finger-pointing voice for a Boston Bruins coach, and he had the looks of one certain animal. Don Adams looked like a penguin! No doubt about it.

Born April 13, 1926, not at the North or South Pole, but rather in New York City, Don Adams started his show business career in the 1950s as a nightclub comic, but his earnings were such that he had to support himself as a commercial artist. He was a good one, but his show business talents proved to be even greater. He had a very special way with impersonations, not so much capturing the voice exactly as capturing the entire character.

Don Adams, perfect for a penguin

One of his personal favorite imitations was a somewhat exaggerated version of William Powell as he appeared in the famous *Thin Man* movies, co-starring Myrna Loy.

And it was this voice that he would eventually use in Buck and Chet's educational series.

In 1962, Don's only regular role on TV had been Perry Como's *The Kraft Music Hall*, where Buck and Chet had seen him, but he had been a guest on many series including *The Steve Allen Show, The Lux Show with Rosemary Clooney, The Chevy Show, The Ed Sullivan Show, The Garry Moore Show,* and even *Playboy's Penthouse*.

And always, he looked like a penguin. Very quickly, this made everything fall into place for Buck and Chet's educational concept. Don's William Powell "we-have-to-win" kind of voice made it clear that he had something he was determined to overcome. And since he was a penguin, it seemed obvious that what he wanted to overcome was being an animal or, more particularly, being non-human. What this penguin was determined to do was prove to the world that he was *just as good as any human being*. Voila! They had it. They had the reason for the desperate need for education, for the "can of spinach." This penguin desperately needed education in order to prove he was just as good, just as capable, as any human.

At this point in their work, word came from Eli that Tom Moore at ABC wanted an extension of his "get-back-to-you" date and asked that the pilot be sent to ABC for showing to other executives (primarily, it seemed certain, to the head of kid programming). Was this a good sign or a bad sign? No one was certain.

Buck and Chet returned to their educational series. Their penguin had to have a partner. Even if they had not wanted this for a myriad of other reasons, the Don Adams voice made the need for a partner perfectly clear. He had to have someone to order around. "All right, Freebish, let's learn how to put that puck where it belongs."

Searching for the partner, their first thought was a seal—the comic flapping of the flippers, balancing a ball on his nose, etc. They were particularly intrigued by the variety of seals called sea lions. "We had a lion star in our first series, so how about another kind of 'lion' in our second?"

Ultimately, they found more ready humor in another polar creature, the ivory-tusked walrus, a fun-loving, somewhat bumbling, laugh-provoking walrus. He seemed the perfect foil for a bossy penguin. In the beginning, the plan was that the walrus would not be able to speak intelligibly. He would only be capable of making peculiar mumbling sounds which the penguin would have to interpret, thereby creating this kind of scene from a first crack at a script:

MECHANICS

          (THE WALRUS IS INSIDE THE CAR. THE PENGUIN IS OUTSIDE AT THE FRONT OF THE CAR, REPAIR TOOLS IN HAND)

WALRUS: Mumble, mumble, mumble, mumble.

PENGUIN: What's that you say?

WALRUS: Mumble, mumble, mumble, mumble.

PENGUIN: Oh, I see. The steering wheel has been stolen.

          (PENGUIN WALKS AROUND THE CAR, THEN POINTS AND SHOUTS)

PENGUIN: You Bubblehead! You're sitting in the backseat!

This seemed a great way to make use of Don Adams' stand-up comedy technique, but very soon it proved too limiting (and tiring) in terms of a partnership. The walrus got his own voice.

(Although they discarded this concept now, they did find a way to use it in a secondary series they originally hoped might be a part of the educational half-hour. This was *Go Go Gophers*, which starred the Gopher Indians: Ruffled Feather and Running Board. Ruffled Feather spoke excitedly in a kind of "hubba-gubba-dooba-gubba" language that was meaningless to everyone but Running Board. He interpreted for viewers. The concept worked well here. Also starring in *Go Go Gophers* was Colonel Kit Coyote, voice and countenance of Teddy Roosevelt as a Rough Rider, and his Sergeant, voice and countenance of John Wayne. It was so successful that it eventually headlined a half-hour series of its own.)

Teddy Roosevelt as a Rough Rider, the model and voice (imitated) for Colonel Kit Coyote.

Actor John Wayne, the countenance and voice (imitated) chosen for the Sergeant on Go Go Gophers.

So, it was established that the penguin and the walrus, in order to prove that they were just as capable as human beings, would leave their residence—a zoo, of course—and go out in the world to get a job: auto mechanics, weathermen, plumbers, whatever. Often they would be unable to get such jobs without help (education), but even if they did, they would quickly get into such deep trouble that failure, if not oblivion, seemed inevitable. They would have to go to someone for assistance.

At an earlier stage, this would have led the heroes to an absent-minded magician, but with the steps that had been taken in terms of transformation, it now seemed wrong to use the kind of "magic" they had first had in mind—to learn about the telephone by having the heroes *become* Alexander Graham Bell and his assistant, to learn about plumbing by having them *become* drops of water or a plunger. This would be so far removed from classroom learning that it was not likely to make kids more friendly toward education, and this is what Buck and Chet wanted.

What they needed was simply a great teacher, an enthusiastic teacher, one who would literally throw himself into the job. And so they created an information imparter who, although not an absent-minded magician, did often forget where he had put things, such as the magical, marvelous, mysterious 3D-BB, a blackboard which was three-dimensional and could offer figures and pictures in motion.

An excitable, information-loving "teacher," this character had a voice and demeanor much like that of actor Frank Morgan's characterization of the slightly inept traveling fortune teller in *The Wizard of Oz*.

That was it - that was the cast and the basic storyline. The penguin and the walrus, breaking out of the zoo to prove themselves, would soon find their future hanging by a thread because of villains like bank robbers or irate housewives or TV viewers unhappy with a weather report. In desperate need of information to get them "out of their tree," they would hurry to the home of the man with all the answers, get their "can of spinach," and save the day.

As for names, once again it all began with the choice of Don Adams as the hero. Because they saw him as a penguin, Buck and Chet had immediately been given half of his name: "Tuxedo." It was too obvious and too delightful to ignore. And what about a first name? They wanted a name with "topspin." In letters received from fans of *The Hunter*, part of the *King Leonardo* series, Buck and Chet had learned that having a character-name which kids might see or hear in some other context could provide meaningful free promotion. Several fans had written that whenever they read or heard about a *hunter*, it made them think of *The Hunter* on *King Leonardo and His Short Subjects*.

To capitalize on this knowledge and on the memorability of alliteration, Buck and Chet chose "Tennessee" for the penguin's first name. This would mean that the new hero would be advertised and promoted every time kids read about the state of Tennessee in their geography or history books or even in newspapers and when they heard about the state on television.

Actor Frank Morgan, the model and voice (imitated) for Phineas J. Whoopee, the man with all the answers.

Tennessee's partner, because he was the hero's chum, became simply, "Chumley." And the information-loving, somewhat absent-minded teacher became "Mr. Whoopee." Why? Because this was the way he often responded when answering questions from Tennessee or Chumley.

"And *whoopee!*" he would shout, "the telephone worked! For the first time in history, a voice was heard over a wire."

One especially memorable piece of business Buck and Chet gave Phineas J. Whoopee was what is known in animation as a "cheat." They gave him a closet like the one listeners had loved for years in the old radio series, *Fibber McGee and Molly*. Week after week on that show, Fibber would go to his closet to find something he needed, and the moment he opened the door, listeners would be treated to an endless avalanche of "things" falling from the overcrowded closet.

What made this particularly great for television was that as soon as Mr. Whoopee began opening the closet door, the picture on the TV screen shifted to Tennessee and Chumley as they reacted to the tremendous number of things falling from the closet. In this way, the cost of animating all those falling items could be "cheated" by having the picture show only the heroes' reaction. Kids loved it.

The use of "Mr. Whoopee's closet" came about because of research Buck and Chet conducted in local schools. Research with kids is often tricky because they tend to tell the researcher what they think he wants to hear. But by showing several different short films and monitoring the kids while they watched, it was possible to discover their favorite comedy element. Buck and Chet labeled it "The P Factor," with "P" standing for predictability. What kids liked best were the moments when they knew what was about to happen.

It was this fact, of course, which made it possible for networks or TV stations to repeat successfully the same kid shows many times. But even when the show was new, when kids were seeing it for the first time, they liked it best when they knew what was about to happen. It seems that O. Henry would never have made it writing kid shows. They do not like surprise endings.

This was a key fact Buck and Chet would remember in creating and writing a new series, especially *Tennessee Tuxedo and His Tales*. The "P Factor" was much in evidence in the pilot script, "Mixed-Up Mechanics." Here, Tennessee and Chumley escape from the zoo to answer an ad for auto mechanics. Hired, they quickly and comically discover their serious lack of knowledge when a machine-gun-toting hoodlum named Rocky Monanoff pulls his car into the garage and demands that the motor be put in perfect condition by three o'clock *or else*! Unable to do the job, and terrified of Rocky, the heroes hurry to Mr. Whoopee who, finding his marvelous 3D-BB in the ever-crashing closet, gives them the basic facts about how an auto engine operates.

Before Mr. Whoopee can complete his information, the heroes race off to repair the engine. "Tennessee Tuxedo will not fail!" insists the penguin. Sure enough, they do manage to get the engine in shape, but when they try to back out the car—yeowwwww!—they discover they have no control. With the gun-toting Rocky Monanoff due any minute, the heroes race back to Mr. Whoopee and learn how the motor must be connected to the wheels. Back at the garage, they have the car ready just as Mr. Monanoff arrives - precisely at the moment Chumley is backing his car out of the garage, and— yeowwwww!—Chumley knocks Mr. Monanoff to the ground with the car.

"Good work," shouts Sergeant Badge, the policeman who just happens to be searching for Tennessee and Chumley. "You've caught the desperate bank robber, Rocky Monanoff! Congratulations!...Now let's get you back to the zoo where you belong."

With the script and character summaries in hand, Chet met with Joe about models and the pilot storyboard, and Buck sat down at his ebony piano to create the theme song for this new series:

> "Come on and see, see, see
> Tennessee Tuxedo,
> See, see, see
> Tennessee Tuxedo.
> He will be
> Parachuting for your pleasure,
> Sailing seas in search of treasure,
> Anything so he can measure
> Up to men,
> That's Tennessee Tuxedo,
> A small penguin
> Who tries but can't succeedo.
> Though he may fail
> As he vies for fame and glory,
> Still he tries in each new story-tale.
> That's Tennessee Tuxedo and His Tales."

In addition to Tennessee, Chumley and Mr. Whoopee, the initial show presentation would include backgrounds of some other important characters:

Stanley Livingston

This is the zookeeper, forever being upset by the illegal absence (or mischief) of Tennessee and Chumley and sometimes others in the zoo. Looking and sounding much like film actor Franklin Pangborn, Mr. Livingston does all he can to hold onto his dignity as his patience is continually tried. (Voice eventually provided by Mort Marshall.)

Flunky

When he can be found and awakened, Flunky is Mr. Livingston's much-needed assistant. Unfortunately, Flunky usually assists only in making his boss more upset than ever. (Voice eventually provided by Kenny Delmar.)

Yak

A two-ton character Tennessee occasionally talks into coming along with him and Chumley in their endeavors to prove themselves. Tennessee might try to take Yak along more often were it not for the fact that his constant yakety-yaks are more than Tennessee can bear. (Voice eventually provided by Kenny Delmar.)

Baldy

An eagle who has also been known to go along with Tennessee and Chumley for one reason or another. For example, he is brought along for the Flying School episode because it is assumed that Baldy has some experience in this field. He doesn't. He might be brought along more often, but he—especially his voice—is a bit depressing, reminiscent of character actor Ned Sparks. (Voice eventually provided by Mort Marshall.)

Sergeant Badge

A policeman who sometimes simply wanders into adventures and sometimes is called into them by Mr. Livingston to search for Tennessee and Chumley. His moments of exasperation remind one of the actor Edgar Kennedy. (Voice eventually provided by Kenny Delmar.)

The theme, the script, the basic plot, the characters—they had it all. The "whole ball of wax" had fallen into place almost the moment Buck and Chet had decided on Don Adams as the hero for their series. And this was why, a year-and-a-half later, Chet pounded on Buck's car outside the 1812 House and suggested they might be able to do the same thing with the superhero series: Choose an actor who could be their superhero—voice and persona—and maybe the rest would fall into place.

Fifteen

Driving from the 1812 House to Cape Cod (Route 12 to 128 to 3), Buck thought about Chet's suggestion. Could they do for their superhero series what they had done for the educational series simply by finding the "star"?

It sounded like a good idea, but could it be done? After all, finding Don Adams had been simply dumb luck, a happy coincidence. Could they do on purpose what they had done accidentally? Could they look for and locate an actor who would supply both the voice and the appearance for their star?

Buck smiled at the question because it seemed to him that the process would be a little like going to a police station and looking at mug books to locate a criminal you had never seen before. Not an easy job.

This was a hot, humid day and, because the little Renault had no air-conditioning, all the windows were open. This created a sound like a small tornado, not terribly conducive to creative thought. Buck cursed this yellow car. If it wasn't blowing all over the damn highway like a leaf, it was making a noise like a wind tunnel.

This was a curse Buck would later regret, for this trip home would prove to be the last the little Renault would make under its own power.

Buck tried to ignore the noise and concentrate on the problem. All that came to him was a discussion he and Chet had had about their superhero's physique. They didn't want Charles Atlas, they decided. Instead, they wanted the 98-pound weakling who normally got sand kicked in his face. That seemed funny already: a 98-pound superhero.

During that discussion, the only name that came up was Don Knotts, who was playing Barney Fife on *The Andy Griffith Show*. In view of this commitment, they doubted he would be interested, but even if he was, his voice was not distinctive enough for the kind of cartoon character they were after, and as for his appearance, that would make the cartoon hero end up looking a little too much like another Don Adams character. They did not want a superhero who resembled "Tennessee."

Okay. Cross out Don Knotts. Who else? Where were the mug books? Could you really search for anybody without knowing what they looked like? Buck sighed. Anyhow, he thought, finding Don Adams had not been a cure-all. Sure, it had brought the show into focus, but it had not solved everything. Not by a helluva lot. Now he laughed at the memory of the first *Tennessee* presentation.

Soon after the *Tennessee* pilot script had been completed, Buck and Chet had gone to Manhattan for a meeting with Eli and Pelican about *Parrot Playhouse*. Despite the most successful sales presentation in their history, Buck and Chet had been advised that the final word from ABC was negative. There was conjecture that this might have come about because they had ignored the head of kid programming and gone directly to the ABC president, but a more likely scenario seemed to be a shift of power. Only days after their presentation to ABC, the man at the top—the man responsible for Tom Moore's presidency—had resigned. This may have left Moore's future in doubt and jeopardized all projects in which he had been involved.

Whatever the reason, ABC's answer was no. This required a meeting at Pelican to discuss the next step for *Parrot Playhouse*. Knowing they were coming into New York, Buck and Chet phoned Gordon, and when they mentioned that the educational series was almost complete, he got very excited and insisted on a personal presentation while they were in New York.

"Give us another week," said Chet. "We'd like to have a finished board for you."

"Forget that," said Gordon. "It doesn't matter whether it's finished or not. I just want to hear about it. Hell, I've been in this business too long to worry about what stage I see stuff."

Buck and Chet could hardly say no, but after what would happen at that meeting, they would never—never, never, never—present a new property, especially a highly *unique* new property—a ground-breaking property—until the entire presentation was in absolutely perfect shape.

At Pelican that morning, it was agreed that *Parrot Playhouse* should be pitched immediately to the other two networks, but there was no doubt that chances for a sale had been greatly diminished by ABC's flat turn-down. There was considerable bemoaning and finger-pointing about the fact that ABC had been give a period of exclusivity. "It never buys you anything," said a member of Pelican, "and it can cost a helluva lot." Eli pointed out that such a request coming directly from the president of the network was very difficult to turn down. It was agreed that, without waiting for answers from NBC and CBS, initial contacts should be made with a syndicator.

Later, in the Gamecock "meeting room" with Gordon, Buck and Chet explained their educational concept—a "can of information"—then used a rough storyboard from Joe Harris to tell the first story. They explained that the figures on this board were meant to show only how the action would work, not how the characters would look, yet—unbelievably—as they began going through the story, Gordon's only comment—not once or twice or three times, but over and over and over again—was, "The penguin's nose is much too big."

Although they explained again that this was only a rough board and that appearances should be ignored, only moments later, Gordon would say, "The penguin's nose is much too big."

It sounds almost absurd, but it was not funny—not to Buck and Chet—because it came very close to shutting down Gordon's mind in terms of how great this series could be. This was why Buck and Chet vowed never again to show unfinished artwork to anyone, no matter how knowledgeable they claimed to be. Better to show no drawings than to show them in the rough.

Despite this major stumbling block, they managed to return to the theory behind the episode and convince Gordon of the merits of the concept, and not just for an inner segment of a show, but to headline a half-hour series. By the time the Gamecock meeting ended, Gordon was sufficiently enthusiastic to ask for a presentation that would include finished storyboards for two nine-minute *Tennessee* episodes, plus the standard opening and closing, plus a good demo of the theme.

Buck and Chet left that meeting with high hopes for *Tennessee*, but just as success seemed to bring them more success, so failure seemed to bring them more failure. The downturn in the fortune of *Parrot Playhouse* was soon matched by a downturn in the fortune of *Tennessee Tuxedo and His Tales*. By the time Gordon's request had been fulfilled—two finished boards, the opening and closing and theme—things had changed at General Mills.

"There's no point in presenting it now," Gordon insisted on the phone. "The situation has changed. The Mills has some major problems, and there's no interest in the educational idea."

"But they *asked* for a series," said Buck.

"No, no," said Gordon. "At the most, they asked to see an idea for a segment. And right now, I don't think we could sell that."

"So what do we do?"

"We wait; wait until the time is right again."

When weeks had passed with no call to action, they talked with Gordon again, but nothing had changed.

"The climate's wrong," he told them. "We go in there now, we won't sell a series; we won't sell a segment. We have to wait for Cy to tell us when the education idea is hot again."

So adamant was Gordon about waiting that he sanctioned TTV's suggestion that *Tennessee* be presented to other possible buyers (corporations with kid products) while waiting for the "climate" to change at General Mills. Three such presentations were made, but, although *Tennessee* was enthusiastically received, there were no takers. Even though the companies were pleased by the idea of winning brownie points with parents and the FCC for delivering education on TV, that same word—education—frightened them off. They admired the originality of the concept, but were not convinced it would deliver high ratings.

Clearly, the best hope for a sale lay with the company which had commissioned an educational series (or, at least, a segment) in the first place. And even if the climate was not right at the moment, this need not stop Gordon from lobbying the series with Cy and others at the Mills, nor prevent Buck and Chet from doing the same with DFS executives who were responsible for General Mills products.

Along the way, Don Adams was locked up for the leading voice role. It may seem strange that he had not been contacted before, but there were two reasons. First, his agreement was not essential. Exceptional voice actors like Allen Swift and Jackson Beck could, after only an amazingly brief amount of time, imitate almost any voice they heard. So if Don said no, a similar voice could be created.

On the other hand, since the participation of a well-known comic would have promotional value, it was best to wait awhile before bringing the matter up with Don. Although he had not yet headlined a series of his own (*Get Smart* was more than three years away), Don was a very successful comic with a great deal of TV experience. If he were contacted while the new series was little more than a creative group's dream, he was not likely to be interested. So they waited until the *Tennessee* presentation was complete and several key General Mills executives had been, at least to some extent, pre-sold. Then they made the offer to Don, and he said yes (especially after he learned he could record his lines "wild," in whatever city he happened to be).

Four months later, after a change of climate at the Mills, *Tennessee* was presented as a half-hour series and, despite Gordon's misgivings, it was snapped up with only one dissenting vote. (CBS had already expressed their willingness to schedule the series on their network.) Meanwhile, *Parrot Playhouse* was rejected by CBS, NBC and three syndicators. Such are the ironies of the TV business. One year earlier, it had seemed absolutely certain that *Parrot Playhouse* would be bought by ABC and rushed to the screen, while everyone involved had serious doubts about whether or not an educational series could ever be sold for competitive kid time. Now, a year later, *Parrot Playhouse* would never be seen on any screen except for presentations, while *Tennessee Tuxedo and his Tales* was sold and would go on to become the only educational series in history to win higher ratings than its strongest competition.

But that would not happen until September of 1963. At the moment, while Buck drove toward his Cape Cod home some two months earlier, *Tennessee* was supplying nothing but headaches. The signed contract with General Mills had only been the signal for everyone at the Mills and at DFS to begin worrying about the content of future *Tennessee* episodes.

Before that contract had been signed, General Mills had insisted on seeing 24 episode summaries (in addition to the two pilot scripts already presented). Such summaries had never been a problem with *King and Odie, The Hunter* or *Tooter Turtle*, but now, because something quite new had been added, every word of every summary was being dissected like a laboratory frog. That "something quite new" was education, and everyone, it seemed, had suddenly become an educational "expert." And if that were not bad enough, General Mills decided to hire *outside* educational experts to review *Tennessee* summaries and scripts.

Since such consultants could earn their fees only by finding fault with whatever they were given to review, Buck and Chet knew that their time would be spent not only in writing their weekly quota of scripts and working on new series, but also in responding endlessly to consultants about what should properly be called education. And they were right. Time and time again, it was necessary to make lengthy phone calls or write lengthy letters explaining how a particular plot summary could be turned into what the consultants called "a true educational experience."

Not until the series would go on the air and clobber its competition would this barrage of educational sniping finally end, but there was one letter from Chet which did help to slow the flow a bit. It responded to a phone call from a member of the DFS who had relayed the negative comments expressed by the General Mills educational consultants regarding *Tennessee* episode #18, an episode which had Mr. Whoopee explaining to Tennessee and Chumley how to build a log cabin. Chet's letter read in part:

> Dear Hotch:
>
> Since we have nothing in writing, it is a little difficult to discuss the consultants' suggestions, but as I understand it, there were basically three, so let's take them one by one.
>
> First, they thought the subject matter was not "educationally worthwhile." Frankly, this puzzles me. The log cabin has played a major role in the history of America. It is the classic symbol of the early pioneers. As the country moved west, the log cabin went with it. In any event, the episode in question will explain to the children how the dwelling place of their forebears was constructed, and if that's not educational *and* worthwhile, I'll eat my hat. As you probably know, there is a progressive school of thought in modern education which holds that nothing is *worthwhile* teaching unless it has some "practical" value, and a battle has been waged over this for years. Now admittedly, there may be no practical application for knowing how to build a log cabin, but we happen to believe that it is *very* worthwhile to teach our children about a part of their American heritage.
>
> The consultants also specifically mentioned that the first step in building should be to "make a plan" and not, as we have it, select materials. It is certainly arguable from an architectural standpoint which comes first, because the nature of the material in a very real sense control the plan—

a building made of steel is designed differently from one of wood. But what is even more germane is the fact that a log cabin is such a simple structure that it requires no plan. I somehow doubt that Abe Lincoln's father had a set of blueprints for his cabin.

Secondly, they felt that the educational portion would not be interesting or amusing. We respectfully submit that this is an area where educational consultants do not belong, and that their comments resulted from a lack of creative imagination. You know yourself how difficult it is for even professionals to envision the final script from a summary. For the untrained to do this is virtually impossible. And even beyond the script, music, sound effects, voice characterization and visual action are all part of making a film interesting and amusing. A judgment formed without understanding all these factors is valueless. I'm sure the consultants meant to be helpful, but they are really in no position to judge whether the educational segment in question will be interesting and amusing or not.

Thirdly, they stated that such an episode could encourage children to chop down trees. I don't know whether to laugh or cry, but I just can't take this comment seriously. Could anyone seriously believe that one Saturday morning cartoon about building a log cabin is going to send even one kid in America rushing out to commit mayhem among the maples? Comments such as this hardly warrant a reply except that I'm afraid that if we let it go by, our lives are going to be made even more miserable as we waste tremendous amounts of time responding to this sort of thing. The episode on coal mining will be said to encourage kids to dig up the lawn, the episode on mechanics will encourage kids to take apart the family car, the episode on the giant clam will encourage kids to run away to sea. But more important, if we don't nip this sort of thing in the bud, truly interesting ideas are going to be eliminated and the whole series weakened.

Regards, Chet

Yes, indeed, Buck was thinking as he drove across Bourne Bridge to Cape Cod, maybe everything had fallen into place for the educational series once they had chosen Don Adams as the star, but that had certainly not been the end of their problems.

Still, Buck would be very happy if they could take that same step with their superhero concept. *Very* happy. But where the hell could they find their 98-pound hero? Buck had been driving for almost two hours, and except for Don Knotts, not one possibility had popped into his mind. Maybe the actor they wanted simply did not exist.

This is how Buck's drive home ended—no candidate for the role of superhero and no hope of finding one. And then, just three days later, there appeared another of those Rod Serling "signposts" that made the birth of Underdog so extraordinary: A movie titled *Spencer's Mountain* arrived in local theaters. The film starred Henry Fonda (his only movie released in 1963), and would eventually spawn the highly successful, long-lived TV series, *The Waltons*. One of the supporting players in *Spencer's Mountain*, listed last in the credits, was an emaciated-looking 39-year-old actor named Wally Cox.

His first lines in the film were: "I was a devotee of Isaac Walton when I was but six. A century or so ago, he wrote *The Complete Angler*."

He spoke slowly and carefully, as if reciting poetry, and he looked very much like a 98-pound weakling who might often have had sand kicked in his face.

Actor Wally Cox, the model and voice for Underdog.

Sixteen

Where could they find a 98-pound weakling? Wally Cox, of course. It was one of those perfect fits which always produced the same question: Why hadn't they thought of it before? Which is why, when Buck and Chet spoke on the phone the week of July 7, there was instant agreement the minute Wally's name was mentioned. In both voice and appearance, surely no more perfect actor could be found.

He was born December 6, 1924, in Detroit, Michigan, but educated in New York at CCNY and NYU. After service in World War II, Wally operated a men's jewelry store in New York, but he told such funny stories at parties that his theatrical friends, including former schoolmate Marlon Brando, insisted he ought to try show business.

Finally, in 1948, he made his comic debut at the Village Vanguard nightclub and won rave reviews. TV guest appearances followed, and in 1949 he became a regular on a DuMont variety series titled *The School House*. The show lasted only four months, but Wally found much more long-lived success in 1952 when he starred in *Mr. Peepers*, a prime-time series on NBC. Wally played a slow-moving, shy, unworldly teacher of science. (The series also starred Tony Randall, later of *Odd Couple* fame.)

Wally's next series, *Hiram Holliday*, also on NBC, had him playing a shy, mild-mannered proofreader at a newspaper who possessed amazing physical and technical skills such as piloting a plane, fencing, scuba diving and art forgery. *Hiram* lasted only five months, and Wally had starred in no other series since then, but had made guest appearances on a wide variety of shows, including *The Garry Moore Show*, *Car 54, Where Are You?*, *The Steve Allen Show*, *Candid Camera*, *The Tonight Show starring*

Johnny Carson, and *77 Sunset Strip*. As of July 1963, his only movie other than *Spencer's Mountain* was *State Fair*.

Wally's personality was much like the one he showed on screen. He was somewhat shy, mild-mannered, slow-talking, kindly and very funny. When he was not working, he enjoyed rock collecting and bird watching. Really.

Buck and Chet knew now with one hundred percent certainty that, whatever kind of animal their superhero might turn out to be, he would look like and sound like Wally Cox. This gave increased importance to the task they had set for themselves in connection with their next meeting: a list of possible names for the superhero or the series.

On the morning of July 10, Chet was so enthusiastic about their prospects for the day that he roared up the Mass Pike from Litchfield and arrived almost thirty minutes early at the 1812 House. Meanwhile, Buck, just as enthusiastic, drove his little yellow Renault so fast that six exits before the one before Route 9 and the 1812 House, something totally unexpected happened.

Not once in all the times they had met to create and write TV series had either Buck or Chet been unable to make the appointment. But now, it seemed that was about to change. Suddenly, it appeared that fog had rolled in on Route 128; very heavy fog; so heavy that Buck was forced to slow down.

But no! That was wrong. This couldn't be fog. It was too black and…it was *smoke*! And it was making its way into the car - the engine was on fire! My God! The engine was on fire. And there was no place to stop in this traffic on 128, even if Buck had wanted to. But wait. There was an exit coming right up, and at the end of that exit there was a large, two-story Buick sales and service center, clearly visible from 128. Buck had seen it many times.That was his only hope.

He managed to get over into the right lane, whipped off the exit, smoke still billowing, and turned left at the end of the ramp. In only seconds, he pulled into the Buick center, took the nearest parking place, turned off the motor and leaped from the car.

Two men from inside, one a mechanic, the other a salesman, had seen the smoking car pull in, and they ran to Buck's assistance. Popping the hood, they used a fire extinguisher to smother the smoke and its cause. Finally, everyone—others from inside had rushed out—breathed a sigh of relief as smoke and flames vanished.

Buck's poor little Renault

Later, the salesman, tall and thin with a crew cut, took Buck into his office. "There's nothing we can do for you in terms of repair. Not with a Renault," he said. "But I really don't believe *anybody* is going to be able to help you with that. My mechanic says all the spark plugs are melted." He shook his head. "How could you keep driving long enough to melt the spark plugs?"

Buck shrugged. "I thought it was fog."

"The smoke? You thought it was fog?" Again he shook his head. "Well, you're welcome to leave that thing here until you...until you do whatever it is you're going to do with it."

"Thanks. And thanks for stopping the fire... Could I use your phone? I just want to call my partner at the 1812 House in Framingham."

Chet arrived in a remarkably short time, and when Buck had thanked everyone in the Buick Center, they got underway. Traffic was not heavy, and Chet soon had the TR-3 up near 70. The top was down, so they had to speak loudly (shout) to be heard above the sound of rushing wind.

"What the hell happened?" Chet asked.

"It just…just burned up."

"Was it out of oil?"

"Who knows? It melted all the spark plugs, that's all I can tell you."

Chet was amazed. "It *melted* them? How could you keep driving long enough to melt the spark plugs?"

Rather tiredly now, Buck said, as he had before, "I thought it was a fog."

"What?"

"The smoke, dammit. I thought the smoke was fog, so I kept on driving. And then, when I finally realized the motor was on fire, there was no place to stop on 128. So I drove to the Buick place."

Chet shook his head. "You're lucky you didn't blow up. Is it totaled?"

"I guess so."

(It was. A Cape Cod junk man would eventually pay Buck $35 for the Renault. It would be replaced by Buck's first 4-wheel-drive vehicle, a cream-colored Scout with a red interior.)

Now, Buck said, "I feel kind of sorry for the damn thing, but it wasn't new and I was getting pretty sick of being blown around on the road every time the wind got over five miles an hour." He shook his head. "Let's talk about something else."

They turned onto Route 9 now, traveling through heavily built up areas, much of it business.

Chet said, "Okay, let's talk about Wally. I think we're onto something."

"Absolutely. He can put us on the path we've been looking for…And not a moment too soon."

Chet looked away from the road briefly. "What makes you say that?"

"Time. Gordon said four or five weeks. That means meeting with him at the latest by the week of July 28. That gives us two weeks to do a wrap. And I was beginning to think we weren't going to get diddly."

Chet smiled. "We needed a break, so we got one. Isn't that how it's supposed to work for us?" He laughed.

Buck nodded. "What about name suggestions? Got any hot ones?"

Chet shrugged his shoulders. "I like what I've got, but the truth is, they were all finished before we talked about Wally."

"Mine, too. We'll have to see which ones fit."

Arriving soon at the 1812 House, they would not return to a discussion of their superhero series for several hours. First, they polished the *Tennessee* and *Hunter* scripts they had completed that week, then plotted one more *Tennessee* and two more *Hunters*.

This done, they adjourned to the dining room with all their paraphernalia and waited until their first martinis had been served before exchanging lists of possible names for their superhero or his series. Both Buck and Chet laughed or chuckled as they carefully read each other's list. There were a total 22 separate listings:

Posse Possum	No rustler or bank robber would want this superhero on his trail, for he packs the power of an entire posse. Falls to the ground as if dead to fool villains.
Spam Sade	Could be any kind of animal, but he is a super sleuth who gets his strength from canned spam.
Moleman	Super digger. Sleeps days, catches crooks by night. Can tunnel anywhere.
Hy Horse	Rides the skies, leaping from cloud to cloud, then swoops down on crooks. One weakness: clear skies.
Yule Mule	Chosen and given his powers by Santa Claus so kids' happiness won't be limited to one day a year. Find a kid in trouble and you may find…Yule Mule!
UNO	The number one superhero of the world with the strongest, greatest powers. Could be any kind of animal.
Army Armadillo	This superhero has the power of an entire army. And when not on the offensive, he can retreat into his shell and become invulnerable, no matter what is thrown at him.
Super Sheep	He can pull the wool over any criminal's eyes.
Abby Deer	This superhero's pretend life is a female newspaper columnist answering letters from the lovelorn, but when that special key on the typewriter is hit, she be-

comes superhero Deer Hunt, champion of all love-abiding citizens.

Cum Laude Cow	We have a female superhero! She wins by way of brains, and she knows how to live; milks every moment for joy.
Dominant Dog	It's all a matter of genes for this colossal canine.
Top Dog	Nice, but Hanna-Barbera already have Top Cat.
King Kong	Doesn't seem to fit our 98-pound weakling image, but how about turning King Kong into a superhero, a good guy. How about…
Kind Kong	Or maybe…
Ping Pong	Giant super ape who bounces around the sky, or…
Ring Rong	Japanese ape. Or…
Wing Wong	Chinese ape that flies.
Mister Mars	Could use planets to imply super strength.
Jumping Jupiter	Comes out of the sky to catch crooks. Home is Jupiter. Or…
Mister Mercury	Can change into things to win the battles. Different shapes.
Chameleon Jones	Speaking of change, how about a superhero who can blend in with anything. Or…
Chameleon Schmuck	Same, but is a bumbler.
Wonder Weasel	Put a rat in a cage with a weasel, and the rat gives up without a fight. Wonder Weasel uses this technique on all the rats of the world.
The Lone Raccoon	He already has the mask. He needs a partner. How about Pronto Peccary, a loyal wild pig?
Wonder Wolf	It is not so much his powers that prevail as it is his "pack." Throughout the world, this superhero has a network of brothers, sisters, cousins, friends ready to

assist him.

Ultra Otter	Zooms into the sky off a long toboggan of wet mud. Protects the world from criminals, but loves to laugh. Will pause in the middle of almost anything to hear or tell a joke, and then laugh his head off.
Trump Cardinal	How about birds? This guy is a master magician. All the powers of a super bird combined with those of Mandrake the Magician. If things go wrong, Trump Cardinal can wing it. Or…
Captain Canary	When he leans on the toughest criminals, their response is perfect: They sing like a canary.
Lethal Loon	He may sound a little crazy, but every villain fears him. They never know what he will do.

"I love them," said Buck, when they had both finished reading. "I can really visualize 'Cum Laude Cow'."

"And I can visualize 'Chameleon Schmuck.' But I think we'll have to pass on that one." He was smiling.

"Why?"

Chet laughed. "In Yiddish, 'schmuck' means penis."

Buck laughed with him. "I didn't know that." They laughed again, thinking about it, and Buck said, "Maybe Chameleon Schmuck could change into a frankfurter-shape when he gets his superpowers; zoom through the sky like a wiener-shaped missile."

"And his name would change to 'Hot Dog.'"

"Right, right," said Buck, still laughing. "And every time he won a battle, he'd shout, 'Hot Dog! Hot Dog!'"

"And people would think he was selling frankfurters, and they'd surround him to buy one, and the crooks would always get away."

They laughed and laughed. Finally, Buck said, "Okay. Cross off Chameleon Schmuck."

Chet took his pen and dramatically crossed off that entry.

Buck said, "I guess what we need to do is see which of these names fits with Wally Cox."

Chet nodded. "We do, but right there is what makes the choice of Wally different from choosing Don Adams."

Buck took another swallow of his martini. "What?"

"The minute we saw Don, we knew what he was: a penguin. He looks like a penguin, even kind of sounds like you imagine a talking penguin would sound. But I don't get that kind of feeling with Wally, do you?"

Buck shook his head. "No, not at all. He could be damn near anything…Well, not anything. can't see him as an elephant."

"Or a giraffe."

"Or even a lion. The truth is, I guess, it's easier to figure what Wally's *not* than what he is." He held up the two lists and shook them. "What about these? Could he be any of them?" He puts the lists back on the table.

"Sure," said Chet. "I don't know that any of them are a great fit, but you could make most of them scrawny—Super Sheep or Wonder Wolf. Not King Kong, of course. That would be a bit of a stretch."

"But do you think these lists would be the same if we'd had Wally in mind when we did them?"

Chet thought a minute—took a sip of his drink—then shook his head. "Maybe not. Maybe we'd have shifted our emphasis away from describing the superhero's powers. Get rid of all those words like 'ultra' and 'wonder' and 'super.' They could apply to any superhero, whatever he looked like." He drained his glass and held it up for the waitress to see.

Buck said, "What you're saying is that we've got a superhero who doesn't look like a superhero, so maybe we ought to give him a super name that doesn't sound like a super name. In other words, what we're looking for is a name that describes our 98-pound weakling; describes Wally."

The waitress brought their second martinis. When she had gone, Chet said, "When we talk about a name that fits Wally, aren't we also talking about one that fits the people he's always trying to help? He's a little guy, and he's out to help the little guy, right?"

"Absolutely. He's not trying to save the rich and powerful. He's for the poor, the downtrodden, the underprivileged."

"'Give us your tired, your poor/'" Chet recited, "'Your huddled masses yearning to breathe free/ The wretched refuse of your teeming shore/ Send these, the homeless, tempest-tossed to me/ I lift my lamp beside the golden door/'"

Buck's eyes widened a moment, then narrowed, as he stared at Chet. He took a sip of martini.

"What is it?" Chet asked. "Did my recitation mesmerize you?"

"Let's use it," said Buck.

"What?"

"Poetry. It sounded great, just great."

"You mean our hero—Wally?" Chet grinned and then laughed. "Why, hell yes. Our superhero speaks in poetry. I love it. We'll have a frigging ball writing that."

"A superhero who speaks in poetry. Oh, brother, does that fit Wally Cox or what?"

Chet nodded. "Perfect...So, he speaks in poetry and he's for the poor and downtrodden."

"The little guy. The kicked-around. He's for the people who've always been given the short end of the stick."

"And now they've got their hero," said Chet. "Their champion...But, what the hell is his name?"

Buck lifted the lists again, looked at them a moment, and then shook his head. "There's really nothing here. Not for Wally and not for the poor and downtrodden. And you know something else?"

"What?"

"No topspin. We came up with all these names, and none of them has topspin. How often would a kid read about or hear about Wonder Wolf or Lethal Loon in some other context?"

Chet took the lists and scanned them quickly. "They're not 'Tennessee,' that's for sure." He put the lists back on the table. "You're right. No topspin."

Buck turned up his hands. "Okay, so where are we? We've got a 98-pound superhero who looks and sounds like Wally Cox and who speaks in poetry and who is the champion of the poor and downtrodden. Instead of going after some power name like Superman or Mighty Mouse, we want to find a name that will do three things." He held up his left hand and pulled the fingers down with his right. "Number one, it will describe or at least *belong* with Wally Cox. Okay?"

"Check."

"Number two..." Buck pulled down another finger, "...we'd like to spell out the people our superhero is out to protect. So instead of going for 'Superman' or 'Powerman,' we'd name him something like 'Little Man' or 'Weakman.'"

"Or 'Poorman' or 'Downtrodden Man.'"

"Right."

"Except that," said Chet, taking a sip of his martini, "all those names stink, and not one of them has any topspin."

Buck nodded and pulled down another finger. "Which is number three—topspin. We sure as hell want a name with topspin." He sighed and leaned back in his chair. "I guess we're going to have to take this home as our assignment."

Chet made a note on his yellow pad, talking as he wrote: "Find a name that describes Wally, describes the people he's championing and gives us topspin."

Buck nodded. "It looks like that's going to take some time...and we haven't got a helluva lot."

Chet put down his pencil and lifted his martini glass. "Meanwhile, all those General Mills guys with a frog fetish are already in Jay's camp."

They laughed somewhat sadly and said, "No doubt about it. In *this* contest, we're the underdog."

That last word was not spoken with any special emphasis or even with above average volume, yet it hit the air with the sound of a giant jackpot falling in a slot machine. And Buck and Chet both heard it.

Underdog!

That name described Wally Cox, and it described the people he would champion—the poor and the downtrodden, all the underdogs of the world. And look at the topspin! Kids would think of this new superhero every time they read about or heard about an underdog—on TV or radio or in books or newspapers, especially the sports section.

And, miracle of miracles, this name made it perfectly clear what kind of animal this new superhero had to be. *Underdog!* Could he be a mole or a mule or a possum? Not very likely. Underdog had to be a *canine* version of Wally Cox.

Underdog was born!

Seventeen

Buck and Chet had only two weeks if they were to be on time when they presented their "super" series to Gordon Johnson. It was always important to be ready on schedule in order to avoid any possible concern about their ability to keep up with weekly script orders. So in the next two weeks, Buck and Chet turned up the heat, meeting twice a week at the 1812 House and working the phones. Their aim was to prepare a presentation with such scope that it would knock Gordon out.

They would have no art (better no art than rough art, they had learned), but they would know the series backward and forward, and they would have everything necessary to show the depth of character and the plot potential.

Underdog would have every power known to exist and a few others that were not. He would fly like a bird, swim like a fish, burrow like a mole. He would have x-ray vision, atomic breath and hi-fi hearing. But—a big but—none of his powers would ever be used to kill or destroy anyone, even the deadliest of enemies. With his atomic breath, for example, he would never blow people off of tall buildings to their death. On the other hand, he might very well blow onlookers around quite a bit (accidentally). And bullets ricocheting off his body would cause pedestrians to leap aside with shock, while pieces of plaster or wood, falling as he crashed into a bank to stop crime, would narrowly miss employees and customers, and both people and companies would sometimes be annoyed by the huge holes he made in their homes or offices as he crashed in or out to curb crime.

With all his powers and all his strength, how could Underdog ever truly become the "underdog?" Oh, there would be armies to help create this situation, also a variety of evil inventions that would appear overwhelming even for Underdog. Still, an invulnerable hero can sometimes get in the way of potential plots. Underdog needed an Achilles heel.

Rather than make this something alien to TV viewers, such as Superman's Kryptonite, Buck and Chet decided to choose something which every viewer, whatever age or sex, would be certain to understand: tiredness. Even a superhero with 200 times normal strength would tire if forced to expend *more* than 200 times the normal amount of energy. So, he would grow tired.

Underdog would be prepared for this dangerous eventuality:

> "The secret compartment of my ring I fill
> With an Underdog super energy pill."

Swallow the pill and Underdog would be revived almost immediately. But if he had this super energy pill in his ring, how could tiredness be an

Marilyn Monroe. She turned into a poodle

Achilles heel? Because the ring might be lost or stolen, or the secret of the ring might be discovered and the pill removed! Or someone close to Underdog might borrow the ring or take it to be cleaned or take it for "safe keeping." And the ring or the pill would be found only at the last nail-biting moment.

In order to have someone who would be a natural magnet for exciting stories, they decided to make their female character a TV reporter (in the same way that Superman's Lois was a newspaper reporter). As an ace TV reporter, this character could draw Underdog into crimes she was investigating for her TV station, and she could also be at the center of a second kind of story in which she was kidnapped by villains who wanted to lay a trap for Underdog so they could carry out some heinous crime.

For the name of their ace TV reporter, the plan was to use the name of Buck's beloved silver purebred poodle, Sweet Petunia B., but Buck and Chet felt "Petunia" was a bit too weak and unrealistic for their reporter, so they switched to Polly and used the alliteration "Purebred" for a last name. Their ace TV reporter became Sweet Polly Purebred, to be modeled after a combination of Buck's poodle and Marilyn Monroe.

The other continuing characters in this series would flow out of the method devised for plotting the episodes.

Recent experience with *Tennessee Tuxedo* had taught Buck and Chet the great advantage in having a leg up when it was time to plot new episodes for a series. With *Tennessee*, the selection of new educational material to be used could be decided upon relatively quickly with the use of an encyclopedia index or even the yellow pages of a phone book. And then, once the education was selected—the telephone or the gasoline engine or weather forecasting—they had a marvelous starting point for the plotting of the episode's action. If the automobile engine was to be explained, then what was needed was someone who demanded that their car be in perfect shape by a certain hour. Enter bank robber Rocky Monanoff. And the episode was on its way.

This had not been true with *King Leonardo*. There, each time a new two-part adventure was plotted, it was almost as if a complete new "book" had to be written. With no leg up, considering each new plot was like asking, "What will we write about today?" It could take hours just to get started.

Buck and Chet were particularly anxious to avoid this "What will we write about today?" in the case of Underdog because the stories would be four-parters, rather than two-parters (*King and Odie*) or one-parters (*Tennessee*). This meant longer stories which would have to be more involved, more complex and, perhaps, more difficult in terms of making each of them unique.

To get past this and, simultaneously, avoid questions from Gordon or General Mills about whether or not the Underdog concept would support a long-running series, Buck and Chet devised three different types of Underdog plots, types which would be rotated. They were:

1. Diabolical inventions created by a diabolical inventor who, among other things, wanted to rule the world. Underdog versus a diabolical inventor.

2. The underworld. Gangsters. Thieves. From bank-robbing to counterfeiting to kidnapping. Underdog versus the Head Hood.

3. Other-world confrontations. Villains from outer space or inner space or out of fairy tales. Monsters and witches and aliens and giant apes (they would finally use King Kong here—Fearo the Ferocious—but as a villain). Underdog versus other worlds.

The third category of plots would produce a different villain for each story, but the first two categories called for continuing characters.

As the actor-model for the diabolical inventor, the initial candidate was Boris Karloff. But he was eventually rejected, first because he was simply too obvious and, second, because in terms of the role in which he had been typecast, "Frankenstein's Monster," he was actually the invention, not the inventor. The model chosen instead was the remarkable actor, Lionel Barrymore, in a cross between two of his most famous roles, the irascible Dr. Gillespie in the *Dr. Kildare* films, and the evil H.C. Potter in *It's a Wonderful Life*.

His first name was chosen quickly. Since he was trying to control all the world's people, trying to tell them exactly what to do, then in effect he was playing the "Simon says" game. "Simon says…Go snow!"…"Simon says…Dry up!" Obviously, his first name was "Simon."

Because of his evil character and, once again, to capitalize on the memorability which goes with alliteration, Simon became Simon Sinis-

*Actor Lionel Barrymore, the model and voice (imitated) for the
diabolical Simon Barsinister.*

ter, but the name felt wrong - seemed aimed at a younger audience, too
kid-ish. Magically, it came to life when "bar" was added. Simon Barsinister,
the evil inventor.

To help Simon with his diabolical schemes, he was given a large, lum-
bering assistant with a voice somewhat like that of Humphrey Bogart in
his first big gangster role, *The Petrified Forest.* To emphasize this assistant's
crude manners, his first name would be Cad, and to emphasize his lowly
status, his last name would be Lackey. Cad Lackey, which made him sound
something like the Cadillac of evil laboratory assistants. Cad Lackey.

For the second category of Underdog plots, a Head Hood was needed,
someone to represent the criminal element, the thieves of the world, the
worthless and disreputable—the riff raff. Had the year been 1972 rather
than 1963, Buck and Chet might have chosen for this image a cotton-
cheeked Marlon Brando from *The Godfather.*

Instead, the mention of "riff raff" took them to much earlier gangster
movies and a pin-striped hood played by George Raft. The name was too

perfect to ignore: Riff Raft. (Although Riff's last name was supposed to be spelled "Raft" after his actor-model, it turned up as "Raff" so often that Buck and Chet finally surrendered. "Riff Raff" became the name.)

Unlike Simon and Cad, Riff would be an animal character, and there was little difficulty in deciding which animal. It was lifted from the list of titles originally considered for the superhero:

Wonder Wolf   It is not so much his powers that prevail as it is his "pack." Throughout the world, this ~~superhero~~-(villain) has a network of brothers, sisters, cousins, friends to assist him.

This became the M.O. for Riff Raff, the head hood with a poisonous pack of pilfering pirates spread out around the world, ready to jump at his command.

It was here that the presentation material for "Underdog" ended, the written material which would be discussed with Gordon Johnson and pitched in later presentations as well. But it was not the end of the background material Buck and Chet created for Underdog. To help them in terms of motivation and attitude in future scripts, they went further, carving out a complete background for Underdog, including birthplace, parentage, the origin of his superpowers, and the reason he spoke in rhyme (while his alternate identity, Shoeshine Boy, did not.)

Several times, Buck and Chet considered using this additional material, but the right script opportunity never quite presented itself. The material remained only in their personal Underdog "bibles," and it will be presented for the first time ever in this book.

But that will come later. Right now, we turn to Buck and Chet's 1812 House meeting of July 24, their last meeting before they would present *Underdog* to Gordon. Having completed all their work for the day, including the *Underdog* presentation, they had moved into the dining room and were waiting for the redheaded niece to serve their first martinis.

"I think everything's great with *Underdog*," Buck was saying. "We ought to get Gordon in our corner the minute he hears those three different types of plots."

Chet grinned. "Sweet Polly Purebred is more likely the thing that'll grab him. He likes Marilyn Monroe."

Buck laughed. "You're right about that. Anyhow, I think he'll like the

Actor George Raft, the image chosen for head hood Riff Raff.

show." Buck's expression changed abruptly, became serious. "But we may need more than that. We may need him to *love* it."

Chet heard something beyond the words. "What does that mean?"

"Did you see this week's *TV Guide?*"

The waitress brought their drinks. They thanked her and took a sip of the martinis as she left.

"What about *TV Guide?*" asked Chet. "I don't buy it or read it."

"Okay, Mr. Educational TV. If you *had* looked at this week's *TV Guide*, you would have noticed that there's a show you and Peg might want to see tomorrow night."

"What?"

"Vic Damone's variety series, *The Lively Ones*. He's got the Benny Goodman sextet guesting as well as Red Nichols and His Five Pennies."

Chet shrugged. "Sounds great, but what the hell does it have to do with *Underdog?*"

"Our competition."

"Ward and Scott?"

Buck nodded. "It just so happens that on Vic Damone's prime-time series, which everybody at General Mills will probably be watching, Jay Ward's darling Bullwinkle J. Moose will do an animated Bossa Nova with Vic."

"In prime-time? Bullwinkle dancing? How the hell does Jay manage stuff like that?"

"Contacts, my friend. He's got some great connections. And anyway, Bullwinkle is a helluva character in his own right. People love him."

"I know. So do I."

Buck said, "*TV Guide* gave *Lively Ones* a half-page 'Close-Up' all its own. If you could buy that kind of promotion, which you can't, it would cost a fortune. The point I'm making is, that kind of artistic publicity gives Jay a real head-start on us in this competition."

"I know, I know," said Chet almost angrily. But then, he smiled. "So Ward and Scott are the heavy favorites. Lucky for us. If they weren't, we'd probably never have come up with the name 'Underdog.'"

Buck smiled now, catching Chet's enthusiasm. "Damn right. And we don't care if Bullwinkle dances with Vic Damone on a flagpole in Times Square. Underdog will still kick the crap out of Ward and Scott's frog."

They raised their glasses in a toast.

Eighteen

Thursday, July 30, Buck and Chet were in the Gamecock "meeting room" before Gordon, but only by a minute or two. Right on time, he came through the revolving door, plunging across the room as he always did, this tall, burly man, his right shoulder thrust slightly forward as if he was prepared to knock down anything which blocked his way.

Buck and Chet were sitting together on one side of the booth to make it easier for them to present the *Underdog* material. They rose to shake hands with Gordon, then laughed as the waiter arrived at exactly that moment with three vodka martinis on the rocks. Gordon liked that.

"I see you've still got that damn beard," he said to Buck and they sat down. "What happened to the moustache?"

"You know me, Gordy," said Buck, preferring not to explain once again that he had never had a moustache. He shifted the conversation. "We could've postponed this meeting until we had art, but we figured you'd rather have us stick to the schedule."

"No, no," said Gordon, "you don't have to make any big deal for me. Just fill me in on where you are."

"We've got the whole thing," said Chet, "and it's great. Just great."

They launched into the pitch. As a place for Gordon's eyes to focus, they had brought black-and-white photos of Wally Cox and Marilyn Monroe, and they stood these up at the end of the table and leaned them against the wall. It was very effective.

They went through all the material in detail—the concept, the character summaries and the pilot script. By the time the presentation was over, they were well into their second martini, and Gordon had been laughing from beginning to end. He had no criticism (very rare), especially loved "not plane, nor bird, nor even frog," and kept chuckling and repeating words like "talks in rhyme," "Marilyn Monroe, "Shoeshine Boy," "There's no need to fear." He loved every element and was particularly taken with the three types of plots.

"That 'other worlds' category is great," he said, "because you can do a lot in space. That's big now. Cy likes the idea of space."

He seemed so fired up over the new series that Buck and Chet did something they would probably not have done otherwise. They told Gordon how it was they had finally decided to do a superhero series.

"We had nothing but that one word from you," they explained. "General Mills wanted a 'super' series, you said. No other guidelines. So after floundering around for days and days, we finally decided we'd go with that one word, 'super.' And what could be more super than a superhero. So, you're actually responsible for the creation of Underdog."

That pleased him.

Buck and Chet began putting away the notes they had used for the presentation as well as the black-and-white photographs.

Carefully, Buck asked, "So, how do you think we stack up, Gordy? Do you think *Underdog* will win the NBC time slot over Ward and Scott's frog?"

"*Hoppity Hooper*," said Gordon.

"That's the name?" asked Chet. "*Hoppity Hooper*? Nice alliteration. What does the frog do? I mean, what's the show about?"

Gordon took a swallow of his martini. "Oh, they just sort of travel around the country. There's the frog, Hoppity. He walks on two legs, but he doesn't wear clothes. He has two friends—Waldo. His voice is most distinctive. Jay got Hans Conried to do it. Waldo is a fox. And there's a big bear named Fillmore. He looks like that bear Disney had in his *Uncle Remus* movie."

"Brer Bear," said Chet. "That was Joel Chandler Harris."

"When they travel around the country," said Buck, "what do they do for entertainment…or to make a living? You know what I mean."

"They're sort of con men…or con animals." Gordon laughed at his own "joke." "They have this wagon, and they sell bottles of stuff, like the peddler with a little show to sell his elixir."

"Oh, sure," said Chet. "The old medicine wagon."

"And they have other schemes," Gordon went on. "A lot of times they get run out of town. It's funny, believe me. You know the kind of stuff Jay does."

"Sure," said Buck.

"It's funny," Gordon said again.

"Has the Mills seen it?" asked Buck.

"No, no. All I saw was a rough board. Jay won't be showing General Mills for a few weeks. And your show has to wait even longer. The Mills doesn't want to talk about it until they know how *Tennessee* rates."

"It'll rate right up there at the top," said Buck quickly.

Gordon shrugged. "I sure as hell hope you're right. The point is, you've got plenty of time to get *Underdog* in perfect shape. I want you to make the greatest presentation possible."

"Sure," said Chet. "That's exactly what we'll do."

Gordon was not listening to him. The blank stare made it clear a new thought had come to him. Now, he smiled and looked at them. "You know what you can do? You can write a new *Hunter* script and put Underdog in it."

That past May, General Mills had ordered 26 episodes of *The Hunter*, to be used in *Tennessee Tuxedo and His Tales*.

"Do you mean a spin-off?" asked Buck.

"Sure," said Gordon. "The Hunter is always in need of help, isn't he? So you write this episode where it's not just the Fox The Hunter's up against, maybe there's also some army from outer space. So, The Hunter calls on his friend Underdog. They're both dogs." He laughed at that. "And all of a sudden, we've got an *Underdog* pilot at no extra cost."

Buck said, "It's a neat idea, Gordon, but it wouldn't let Underdog be seen in the same light as if he had his own pilot."

Chet said, "I don't think we could possibly do justice to an Underdog story if we tried to squeeze it into 4:30, especially if we have to include The Hunter."

Gordon shook his head. "You think about this one. You'll be missing a great opportunity if you let this go by. You do this, and Ward will be presenting a storyboard while you can be competing with a film. That could really give you an advantage."

Buck and Chet did their best to counter this suggestion without alienating Gordon, but he was still harping on it when the luncheon was over and they were paying the check.

The spin-off idea had somewhat dampened Buck and Chet's spirits. This meeting had started out so well, with Gordon tremendously impressed by the Underdog material. Then he became caught up in his spin-off idea and said little or nothing more about the merits of *Underdog*, itself.

"I think that *Hunter* spin-off idea stinks," said Buck when he and Chet were alone, walking uptown to the Warwick Hotel. The sun was bright and very, very hot.

Chet nodded. "It's like introducing a new Cadillac by having it pop out of Volkswagen." He turned to Buck. "If spin-offs are so frigging great, why doesn't Jay do one? Why doesn't he spin-off *Hoppity* in a *Rocky* episode?"

Buck shook his head. "Can't. General Mills isn't buying new *Rockys* now. They're out of production."

"Oh."

"Do you think Gordon actually believes we *need* to get Underdog on film if we're going to beat Ward's storyboard?"

"He sounds like it," said Chet, "but if that's Ward's series—three animal characters riding around in a medicine wagon—I don't get it."

"Yeah," said Buck. "Maybe Gordon left something out."

Their gut instinct told them that Gordon, no matter how good his intentions, was wrong on this one. The new series needed to be sold with a one hundred percent *Underdog* presentation, not diluted by another character, especially one who was already as well-known as The Hunter. On the other hand, they did not want to make Gordon think they were ignoring his guidance or make him think they were not doing all they could to come up with the best possible presentation for *Underdog*.

They jotted down a couple of ideas introducing Underdog in a *Hunter* episode so that they would have something to mention in case Gordon brought up the subject on the phone, but they actually continued with Underdog in the way they had planned before the Gamecock meeting.

Joe was already at work on models and the pilot board (even Joe, usually so quick to capture what Buck and Chet had in mind, initially misunderstood what happened when Shoeshine Boy became Underdog. Joe assumed that there would be bulking-up, as if the 98-pound weakling changed into the muscular Charles Atlas. But he quickly got it when Chet explained that the 98-pound Shoeshine Boy simply changes into the 98-pound Underdog. Wally Cox remains Wally Cox.)

Meanwhile, Buck sat down at the ebony piano and wrote what would become one of TTV's most popular theme songs:

"When in the world the headlines read
Of those whose hearts are filled with greed,
Who rob and steal from those who need,
Then to this spot with blinding speed
Goes Underdog...Underdog."
Speed of lightning,
Roar of thunder,
Fighting all who
Rob or plunder
Underdog...Underdog.
When criminals in this world appear
And break the laws that they should fear
And frighten all who see or hear,
The cry goes up both far and near
For Underdog...Underdog.
Speed of lightning,
Roar of thunder,
Fighting all who
Rob or plunder
Underdog...Underdog.

Nineteen

What happened next was another of those Twilight Zone events which occurred so frequently in connection with Underdog. It was not just an event, really. It was a series of events. And although they were all negative, strangely enough they opened a positive door for Buck and Chet, made it possible for them to escape Gordon's spin-off idea without any alienation.

The events concerned *Tennessee Tuxedo and His Tales*. When that show had been presented to General Mills, virtually every executive in the meeting had gone on record as being totally in favor of contracting for this series. But during the period between that meeting and the debut of *Tennessee*, several things happened. There were, first of all, the educational consultants mentioned earlier who registered their concern about not only whether this was the right kind or the right amount of education, but even whether or not it would be entertaining! They did this with episode-summary after episode-summary and then with script after script.

Although Buck and Chet, with Gordon's help, finally managed to dam that avalanche of criticism, by the time this was accomplished, the constant sniping had done damage elsewhere. A very vocal minority of those who had been so quick to register a "yes" vote in the original *Tennessee* presentation began to have doubts about the program's potential ratings, especially as the debut date drew near and they learned that this *educational* series, scheduled for CBS Saturday morning in black-and-white, would have to face, in color, *Ruff and Reddy* on NBC.

This was Hanna-Barbera's first TV series and only the second cartoon show purchased especially for kid TV. Regularly taking its time-period according to Nielsen ratings, this series would be a formidable challenge.

"That show even has its own comic books," said one *Tennessee* doomsdayer. "Something has to be done to strengthen our show. As soon as the kids see that education, they'll be gone to *Ruff and Reddy*."

No matter how many memos from TTV were written and no matter how many times Buck and Chet made the case in person, these executives could not be convinced that kids would stay with Tennessee and Chumley because they would want to see them escape from the trouble they were in.

It was ironic that one of *Tennessee's* most repeated expressions was "Tennessee will not fail," and now the repeated cry from some who had originally endorsed *Tennessee* was, "*Tennessee Tuxedo* will fail." It was as if these executives wanted to get in a position that would allow them to say, if the series failed, "See. I told you."

So overwhelming did this negativity become, that it spread to other work TTV was doing for the Mills—the new *Hunter* episodes, for example. There had never been a problem with any scripts for this character. Now, suddenly, Buck and Chet found themselves defending this series, too. Finally, it was not at all unreasonable for Buck and Chet to tell Gordon that, so concerned were they by the client's negative attitude toward their work, that this did not seem like a propitious moment to lock-in another series with General Mills, and that is what would have happened if *Underdog* were a spin-off from the Mills-owned *Hunter* series. Instead, they told Gordon, TTV would prefer to be in a position where, depending on the Mill's vacillating attitude toward *Tennessee*, the new series could be pitched to other competitors.

It was a rather daring move, but it proved to be one which Gordon Johnson approved of. "Makes sense to me," he told Buck on the phone. "Forget about *The Hunter* spin-off. Move ahead with the *Underdog* presentation just like you pitched it to me. And if General Mills keeps nitpicking, we can try to sell *Underdog* someplace else. But I have to be honest with you. If *Tennessee* does a belly-flop, I don't think you'll be able to sell *Underdog* or any other show to anybody anywhere. At least, not for a long time."

Gordon was probably right. To keep *Tennessee* afloat, TTV had been forced to go out on a limb. Because "education" was such a dirty word in kid TV, in order to keep *Tennessee* from sinking before it was launched, it had been necessary to hammer home again and again that the series would deliver high ratings, virtually *guarantee* that this would be the first educational series ever to achieve high ratings. They had, in other words, been forced to stick their corporate necks out in a very public manner. The result: If *Tennessee* failed, TTV's credibility vanished.

And so it came down to that fateful Saturday morning, September 28, 1963, when *Tennessee Tuxedo and His Tales*, made its debut on CBS. How did it rate? Did the kids run away the moment they saw the education begin? Absolutely not. The show was a smashing success, taking its time period so handily week after week that it captured almost *twice* the share of audience watching *Ruff and Reddy* and did the same thing a year later when NBC changed the competition to a new TV series, *Hector Heathcote*.

A UPI press release about *Tennessee* popped up in newspaper columns all across the United States, like this one in Jack O'Brian's "On the Air" column of March 3, 1964:

> "CBS is fooling youngsters with *Tennessee Tuxedo*. The kids don't realize the show is educational and instructive behind all that cartooning. That's what we call a good clean trick."

The "trick" was not only appreciated by kids, but by educators as well. Many asked for episodes to use in their classrooms for "teaching tools." Especially gratifying to Buck and Chet were higher education letters like the one from A.M. Fortis of the University of California in Berkeley regarding the *Tennessee* episode which featured *simple machines*. Mr. Fortis wrote, "May I have a copy of that episode? I have never seen a more interesting, more lucid explanation. I would like very much to show it to my class."

Tennessee's performance was truly amazing, not only educating while it entertained, but capturing the lion's share of the audience while it did so. It is a feat that has never been repeated by any other program. Many viewers, not fully understanding ratings, may be under the impression that a show like *Sesame Street*, coming to PBS years later, matched *Tennessee*'s accomplishment. But this is far from the truth.

Although *Sesame Street* has much to recommend it, the show has never achieved high ratings; its share of the audience is only a fraction of that captured by *Tennessee*. The fact of the matter is, *Tennessee Tuxedo* reached with its first half-hour episode more children than *Sesame Street* reached in its entire first season.

Even to this day, Buck and Chet meet many adults who tell them, with something of a "you got me" expression, that they never realized they were being educated when they watched *Tennessee*, yet the lessons they learned from the series are ones that have stayed with them more clearly than any others.

Twenty

In the two months prior to the debut of *Tennessee*, work had gone forward steadily on the *Underdog* presentation. The storyboard and theme music had been completed, voices chosen and a final soundtrack recorded. And then, with Gordon's one hundred percent agreement, the storyboard had been transferred to animatic film which would move frame by frame in-sync with the soundtrack. It was the most impressive (and expensive) presentation in TTV history, and Gordon, himself, would take the material to Minneapolis and present it to General Mills.

Ward and Scott's *Hoppity Hooper* had been presented earlier, and it won an excellent reception. As always with Ward's material, there were some very funny lines, and they brought laughter at the General Mills pitch. The only negative comment had to do with the name. There was some fear that it sounded too familiar. There had been, after all, a "Hoppity," a grasshopper wearing a fedora and a green jacket who had enjoyed some feature-length fame in *Mr. Bug Goes to Town*. And later there had been "Hippity Hopper," a baby kangaroo who escaped from a zoo and ended up in the cellar of the home where Sylvester the Cat hunted mice in Warner Bros. short subjects. (A year after Ward's *Hoppity Hooper* debut, the show title was changed to *Uncle Waldo*.)

Gordon waited until he had three weeks of ratings for *Tennessee Tuxedo and His Tales*, ratings which proved conclusively that the show was an overwhelming success, thus giving TTV's image new luster. Then he arrived at the Mills with the animatic presentation for *Underdog*.

It was a splendid success, so much so that on the spot, no doubt whatsoever remained about which series, *Hoppity* or *Underdog*, would win the contest. *Underdog* would debut at 10:00 A.M. Saturday morning on NBC, while *Hoppity Hooper* would be relegated to a much later time slot on the third-rated network, ABC.

About one year later, October 3, 1964, while *Tennessee* was still knocking 'em dead, *Underdog* made his debut to glowing reviews and terrific ratings. The show would run for an astounding nine years on the network, the longest network run for any kid cartoon series in history.

Buck and Chet would buy an airplane and hire a retired Air Force Colonel to fly them to their weekly meetings. They would buy a beach front motel and a string of cottages. And while this was going on, Underdog's most popular couplet would become the cry of kids everywhere:

"There's no need to fear.

Underdog is here!

So they bought an airplane and...

Underdog would become a balloon in the Macy's Thanksgiving Day Parade, have his picture on the front page of the *New York Daily News* (twice) and be on the cover of *New Yorker* magazine. There would be Underdog comic books, children's books, games, puzzles, statues, records and lunchboxes. And every week, kids all over the world would tune to Saturday morning TV to hear:

"Look! Up in the sky!

It's a plane...

It's a bird...

It's a frog...

A frog?"

UNDERDOG: "Not plane, nor bird, nor even frog.

It's just little ole me...Underdog."

THE END

Afterword

BACKGROUND

Although written in 1963 as part of the Underdog "bible" kept by Buck and Chet, the following background material was never presented to DFS or General Mills and never used in *Underdog* episodes. It appears here for the first time.

UNDERDOG

He was born in Huntsville, West Virginia, where his father, Lewis N. Clark, worked as a coal miner. Wages were low and the family of three, living in a small log cabin in a wooded area far from town, had difficulty making ends meet.

His mother, Molly Barker, before she became Molly Clark, helped earn money by writing poetry which was bought by local and regional publications and, occasionally, by national magazines such as *Reader's Digest* and *The Saturday Evening Post*.

Named after his father, the future Underdog was called "Junior" by his parents and by his friends. Although the family was poor, Junior's life was happy and relatively uneventful until he was about to enter high school. At that time, when a dangerous criminal escaped from nearby Fullsome Prison, and everyone in the area was asked to help find him, it was discovered that Lewis was extraordinarily gifted at tracking, finding the path the escaped criminal had taken and discovering his whereabouts under even the most difficult of circumstances.

After capturing the first escapee and then repeating the feat several times, Lewis' fame spread rapidly, and he began to be called upon by prison officials, bail bondsmen, even private individuals suffering because someone close to them had vanished. The elder Lewis might have become wealthy as his fame spread, but he refused to take monetary advantage of his talent.

His tracking freed him from the coal mine, which pleased him greatly because his lungs had suffered there, and a lower level explosion had damaged his hearing. But in terms of fees for tracking, he would take little more than the money he might have earned down in the mine shaft if his tracking talents had not been discovered.

As his reputation grew, Lewis prided himself on the fact that he had never once failed to bring back anyone he had been hired to track. Then, when Junior was 18 years of age, it appeared that his father's perfect record might be spoiled. Lewis was searching for a particularly unpleasant criminal, a fraudulent dentist (no credentials) who had been convicted of pulling healthy teeth and then charging exorbitant prices for doing this totally unnecessary, often very painful, work. The day he had been convicted, he had escaped from a courtroom far from Huntsville.

When Lewis was recruited to bring back this criminal, he was shocked to discover that this dentist had once worked on him! He had removed two teeth, quite painfully, which had almost certainly been healthy. This was the first time Lewis had ever been personally involved with anyone he hunted, and it may have caused him to be over-zealous and perhaps careless.

Chasing the dentist across an unprotected railroad crossing, Lewis' car stalled and, with his poor hearing, he did not hear the approaching train until it was almost upon him. Miraculously, he lived, but only long enough to make a deathbed plea. In the hospital, he asked Junior to finish the hunt, to bring the dentist to justice.

Even as distraught as Junior's mother was, almost destroyed by her husband's death, Molly did not try to stop Junior from going after the dentist. On a stormy night filled with lightning that streaked again and again from sky to ground, Junior picked up the dentist's trail at the railroad crossing and tracked him to a deserted coal mine. It turned out, Junior had not really been tracking the dentist so much as the dentist had been leading him to this mine...to destroy him.

Tricked into going down into the lowest level of the old mine, Junior discovered that the dentist had already made his exit, and now blocked Junior's only way out with an explosion. As if this alone was not enough to finish poor Junior, the dentist began pumping into the mine where Underdog was trapped the "laughing gas" dentists used at that time to ease patients' pain.

At exactly the moment this gas reached the bottom of the mine and filled the space where Junior was trapped, a bolt of lightning struck the mine and raced down the shaft to that room full of gas. What followed was like nothing ever recorded before in history.

The combination of lightning and laughing gas in that small area so far beneath the surface of the earth produced an *unreleased* explosion with a power and pressure of such dimensions that the coal left in this mine was literally turned to diamonds, and Junior underwent a comparable transformation. While he was laughing hysterically due to the huge quantity of laughing gas, Junior's eyes, ears, and muscles underwent a remarkable change, and he was empowered to become "Underdog."

Without full realization of what had happened to him, Junior's first thought as he made his way out of that mine was to keep his promise to his father: bring the dentist to justice. This was not difficult; did not require any of Junior's newly developed powers. So certain had the dentist been that he had finished off this tracker, that he had not even left the premises. Junior captured him quickly, and returned him to the authorities from whom he had escaped. The record of the late Lewis N. Clark remained unblemished.

Back at home, Junior did not immediately speak of what had happened to him, for he and his mother were too caught up in grief, in burying their father and husband. And as weeks passed, Molly seemed unable to recover from this loss. But Junior finally spoke to her—he had to speak to someone—and discussed his new powers.

"It's providence," said his mother almost immediately. "Your father is gone—can no longer track down criminals—and you have been given strengths beyond belief."

"So, what should I do, Mother?"

"Use those powers to do what your father did; use them to fight for right and to help others in need. Use them for good. Help to bring a balance to life, to protect the poor and the helpless, the needy, the underdogs of the world."

And that was how Junior found his new name, "Underdog."

"I understand," he said to his mother. "That's what I'll do."

"But you must never let those powers make you feel better than others. You must keep your feet on the ground, my son. Find a way to help you remain unchanged inside, no matter what fame comes to you."

This was why Junior would eventually adopt the personality of Shoeshine Boy whenever he was not fighting evil or helping others as Underdog. Shoeshine Boy would help to keep Underdog's feet on the ground.

Molly did not live long. There seemed no medical reason for her death. Some said the cause was simply the loss of Lewis; a broken heart. She did not want to continue on without her husband. Whatever the reason, she was gone less than a year after Lewis. And Junior was left alone.

He promised on his mother's grave that he would do as she had asked: Fight for the underdogs of the world and always remain humble. He made one other promise: As the hero of the poor and helpless—as Underdog— he would always speak in rhyme so that each time he spoke, he would be paying homage to his mother.

And, close to his heart, underneath the "U" on his chest, Underdog would always keep the last poem his mother had written.

> Lies are like doors,
> And quickly we learn,
> When doors lock behind us
> We can never return.

Underdog would never lie.

THE UNDERDOG SHOW WAS A REUNION

Because episodes of *Go Go Gophers* were part of *The Underdog Show* when it debuted, the program was something of a voice reunion for two of the actors, Wally Cox as Underdog and Kenny Delmar as Colonel Kit Coyote.

It seems that fifteen years earlier on *The School House*, Wally's first TV series as a regular, he had played a student, and the teacher and *star* of *The School House* had been Kenny Delmar.

THE ONLY REJECTED *UNDERDOG* EPISODE

Only one *Underdog* story was ever turned down by General Mills or DFS. This was one in which Simon Barsinister invented "Truth Paste" and put it in stores all across the country, replacing regular toothpaste. The plot was simple: People would, unknowingly, buy Truth Paste, take it home and brush their teeth and almost immediately, they would begin telling the truth. This would soon make them hate each other and begin fighting like cats and dogs. Simon would take over.

On behalf of General Mills, DFS registered a distinct lack of enthusiasm for this idea. Their objections were based in part on a belief that kids should not be given the idea that telling the truth was a bad thing. But more important, perhaps, DFS did not like the suggestion that Simon (or anyone) could tamper with or exchange products on the shelves of stores.

"Next thing you know," someone suggested, "Simon will be dropping things in cereal boxes to create a *cereal killer*."

The "Truth Paste" story was dropped.

In 1991, there was the very real possibility of selling a sponsor or network on buying a totally *new* Underdog series. Toward this end, Buck and Chet created this presentation.

THE RETURN OF UNDERDOG

When September 21, 1992 arrives, it will have been precisely 25 years since the last *Underdog* episode was completed—a perfect moment to announce the return of the Battling Bard. This will be the first time in history that a Saturday morning TV star has made such a return, and it is fitting that Underdog should be the one to do so, for this will be only another in a long list of "firsts" to his credit.

To mention only a few, Underdog was the first to make the cover of *New Yorker* magazine. He was the first to make the front page of the *New York Daily News*. He was the first to have a successful record made from one of his adventures ("Thanksgiving"). He was the first to have his theme played at sports events by bands across the country (for the school teams which happened to be the "Underdogs"). He was the first to have not one, but *two* nighttime series created in his image. These programs appeared in prime-time in 1967, both of them recognized by viewers and critics and actors (and, in one case, even the creator) as *Underdog* rip offs, because they both had Wally Cox-type heroes who demonstrated the same sort of inept behavior made famous by Underdog. The two copycat series were *Captain Nice*, starring William Daniels and Alice Ghostly, and *Mr. Terrific*, starring Stephen Strimpell and John McGiver. There are many who feel that still a third prime-time series, *The Greatest American Hero*, was patterned after *Underdog*.

But never mind the copies. Imitation remains the sincerest form of flattery, and these pale efforts have done nothing to rob the Resolute Rhymer of his unique credentials. He remains today the only extant superhero whose conduct reflects reality, deluging the onlookers with debris while diving in or out of buildings, and destroying chimneys and TV antennae as his attention is momentarily diverted by the camera. He is also the only superhero who speaks in rhyme, and the only one with a name which delivers subliminal advertising, popping up as it does again and again in conversation, on television, and in magazines and newspapers, especially the sports sections. Everybody loves an Underdog.

PRODUCT & PROMOTION

A magazine cartoon of a year ago had a husband and wife watching Underdog on television. "I wonder why they don't have any *new* adventures of Underdog?" asked the wife. And the husband replied, "He's probably been too busy fighting the Gulf War."

Which brings up the question, where has Underdog been for 25 years? Just imagine what this question (and all that has happened during those 25 years) offered in terms of publicity and promotion opportunities. For example, the answer to the question of Underdog's whereabouts was that he was doing undercover work to help the U.S. win the Cold War. Now that this battle for freedom appears to be behind us, Underdog has the time to return to his more usual occupation as crime-fighter and TV star. Won't that make for some great promotion?

There are excellent trade publicity opportunities in terms of "updating" Underdog adventures with new computer effects for animation, and using electronic musical techniques to enhance the popular theme. Kids can be intrigued with the notion of refloating the Underdog Thanksgiving Day Parade balloon ("Who Shot Down Underdog?") and with finding a voice to replace that of Wally Cox. Obviously, we will have no difficulty locating a voice-man who can imitate the late Wally Cox (we have used one for past emergencies), but if we like, much can be made of finding this new Underdog. It can be a genuine talent hunt—among both teens and adults—ranking right up there as the most exciting talent search since Vivien Leigh won the role of Scarlett O'Hara.

Much publicity and promotion can also be based on the question of what has happened in the lives of the other Underdog characters during the past 25 years. Has Sweet Polly Purebred been promoted? Has her reporting on television won her any awards? What has happened in her personal life? And what of Simon Barsinister, Cad Lackey and Riff Raff? Is Tap-Tap still alive? Also of interest, will there be any new regular characters on the series? A new villain, perhaps, to rival Simon and Raff?

Perhaps most exciting of all, in terms of publicity and promotion, the new *Underdog* series will reveal for the first time the full biography of the Poetic Powerhouse! That's right. Viewers will finally learn what many have pondered for years: Where was Underdog born? Who were his parents? Are they still alive? Where did he grow up? How did he get his amazing powers? Why does he speak in rhyme when he is Underdog, yet speak normally when he is Shoeshine Boy? And what is the basis of his relationship with Sweet Polly? Why above all voices calling for help can he always hear hers: "When Polly's in trouble, I am not slow./ It's hip-hip-hip, and away I go!"

The opportunity to learn the answers to these long-held secrets will be enough to excite the heart of every Underdog fan, young and old alike.

NEW ADVERTISING

So much has happened in 25 years. So much has changed. Almost everywhere we look, past and present and future, exciting ideas for new Underdog adventures are waiting like apples on a tree. We need only pick them.

The 4-part, half-hour stories for Underdog have always fallen into one of three categories and will continue to do so. These are:

1. *Simon Barsinister* Episodes – Built around an invention such as "The Forget-Me-Net."
2. *Riff Raff* Episodes – Built around intriguing thefts such as "The Gold Bricks."
3. *Other Worldly* Episodes – Built around strange creatures such as "The Flying Sorcerers."

Following are thumbnail summaries of nine 4-part stories which quickly come to mind based on fairly recent newspaper items.

SIMON BARSINISTER STORIES

1. *Inner City Gangs*: Simon decides to gain control of the young inner-city gang members to help him take over the world.
2. *Cloning*: One Simon is bad. Two are terrible. But what about ten

thousand! And you can produce them just by talking to Simon on his Clone-Phone.

3. *Hate Mongers*: Simon is marketing a low-priced Hate-Gate. Whoever walks through is filled with hate. When everyone in the world hates everyone, Simon takes over.

RIFF RAFF STORIES

4. *Berlin Wall*: Riff's gang has sold their last piece of the Berlin Wall, and they're broke. Riff will leave no stone unturned to find a new source of wall.

5. *Christo Art*: A famous artist is wrapping the Empire State Building in tissue paper, and they want Underdog to put the bow on top. Surprise! It's all a Riff Raff plot to get Underdog out of the way.

6. *Artificial Reality*: How easy it is to rob bank after bank when all the tellers are caught up in the new artificial reality. And what happens when it is welded onto Underdog!

OTHER WORLDLY STORIES

7. *Face on Mars*: Countries are putting the "face" found on Mars on their stamps. Why should that cause the earth to move in Egypt?

8. *Computer Virus*: This one has the machines actually coughing and shaking with chills due to fever. How do machines use humans to "get well"?

9. *Lumberjacks and Owls*: The argument seems without answer, and now a giant UFO arrives. The "creature" stepping out carries a great axe. It's a new Paul Bunyan! And he's a match for Underdog.

Adding substance to the statement that the uniqueness of the Underdog series makes finding new adventures as simple as picking apples off a tree, let's take three of the above - one in each category—and flesh them out a little.

1. *Inner-City Gangs*

Impressed with the rampage of inner-city gangs, Simon tells Cad he will use these young thugs in his quest to take over the world. He'll become their leader. "But gee, Boss," says Cad, "they won't let a runt like you take over." "Oh, yes they will," says Simon. "I have a new weapon they'll want." And he holds up a short board. When Cad laughs, Simon explains, "It's a plank, you idiot. A Gang-Plank. And it's the greatest weapon in the world!" But when Simon goes before the first gang, they are as unimpressed as Cad. They laugh uproariously and demonstrate their own weapons—machine guns, switchblades, automatic pistols, etc. Then Simon stuns them with a demonstration of his Gang-Plank. He puts it on the floor like a skateboard, gets on and shouts, "Simons says—go, go, go!" And he takes off like a rocket, spinning circles around gang members, finally going so fast he vanishes. He makes their weapons useless, confusing the gang until they spin and fall. "With your youth and my weapon," says Simon to the groggy gang, "I can rule the world!" Can Underdog save the day?

4. *Berlin Wall*

Riff Raff has a huge packaging plant in Idaho ("no small potatoes,") which was used for boxing pieces of the Berlin Wall he and his hoods had ripped off. But, now those pieces of the wall are gone, and what's to be done with this great packaging plant? "What we need," says Riff, "is another wall." The scene shifts to a tour guide in China pointing and saying, "And this, of course, is the China Wall." But it isn't. That part of the wall vanishes right before our eyes. And then another tour guide spots more missing. And another, still more. Soon the Great Wall of China is one-quarter gone, and still vanishing. Sweet Polly Purebred gets the word and tells her viewers the tragic story. All nations are saddened, for this is truly one of the great wonders of the world. The U.N. meets and agrees to call out forces to try and halt the heist and find the missing wall. Meanwhile, in his plant in Idaho, Riff is shocked by all the commotion. "I don't get it," he tells his boys. "They didn't move a finger when we took the Berlin Wall. What's so great about China?" For protection, Riff uses the new stone to wall-in his packaging plant while he continues to get the new product ready for market. When Shoeshine Boy spots a new item in stores marked "China Wall," he becomes suspicious, and Underdog goes into action. Unfortunately, Sweet Polly has been investigating on her own and has been captured by Riff at his Idaho plant, a real hot potato for Underdog.

7. Face on Mars

We see stamps being turned out by several countries, each excited by the possibility that the "face" photographed atop a pyramid-like structure on Mars is actually man-made. Congress has just authorized funds for a manned expedition to Mars to determine once and for all if living beings produced that Sphinx-like face. While our camera is on this face of the stamp, we do a match-dissolve to an almost identical face, except that some of the nose is missing. We have dissolved to the Sphinx in Egypt, and the ground is shaking. Unbelievably, the Sphinx stands up and begins to move! People scream and yell in fear, and some foolishly fire shots at the stone image. Now the Sphinx is moving forward, first slowly, but then faster and faster, eventually racing across the desert, crushing cities, leaping seas and then, shockingly, leaping the Atlantic Ocean! Underdog is called as the Sphinx marches on Washington. The Resolute Rhymer wins a vicious battle, but suddenly a *second* Sphinx pops up where the old one was in Egypt. And then, one by one, a whole army of Sphinx appear, an army that soon heads for Washington. The U.S. Army and Navy prepare for battle as Underdog, with Sweet Polly's help, discovers that the Sphinx was programmed thousands of years ago to protect the Face on Mars. How can Underdog use this shocking information to defeat the army of Sphinx and save America?

IN CLOSING

A character and series loved by millions, endless opportunities for publicity and promotion, and more stories than you can shake a stick at. Could anyone ask for more than this—the exciting return of the Valiant Versifier, new challenges for the Poetic Powerhouse, super-sized heroics for the Resolute Rhymer? Thank heavens! At long last we will all be able to look up into the sky and ask once again, "Is it a plane? Is it a bird? Is it a frog?" And the Battling Bard can respond once more: "Not plane, nor bird, nor even frog./ It's just little ole me—Underdog."

Unfortunately, the "Return" never materialized.

A NEW 1:30

All of the General Mills-owned cartoon series, from *Rocky* to *Underdog*, contained a 1:30 show element. This was needed in order to create an extra commercial position. The first 1:30 starred Bullwinkle as "Mr. Know-It-All." The second series of 1:30s were "The Adventures of Twinkles."

In early 1964, with the Twinkles brand of cereals being phased out in grocery stores, it was agreed that the pink elephant's adventures should be eliminated from the General Mills shows, especially since the Twinkles stories, geared to a younger audience of kids, had never been a help to ratings.

In mid-March, Gordon Johnson asked Buck and Chet to come up with a new 1:30 series geared to older kids. This assignment was particularly important because these new episodes would be used for the September debut of *Underdog*, and even perhaps in *Hoppity Hooper*.

It was a tougher assignment than might be supposed by anyone not in the business of creating cartoon series. Payment for cartoon material from General Mills was based in large part on length, meaning that for these new 1:30 episodes, Buck and Chet would be paid little more than one-third what they were paid for a 4:30 episode of, say, *The Hunter*. But unless they were very careful, the plotting and writing would take far more than one-third time and effort required to complete a *Hunter*.

Without the right format, they would begin the plotting of each 1:30 episode with little more than a blank sheet of paper, and this would mean the investment of an amount of time almost equal to that required for an episode of *The Hunter* or *Go Go Gophers*.

To avoid this, they looked for some broad concept that would allow them to use a wide variety of material from a wide variety of existing sources. They found this in the idea of *Tall Tales*, a simple formula which could utilize all the large exaggerations (lies) they had ever heard or read or could dream up. Each episode of this series would simply flesh-out one large lie.

As their continuing fabricator, the hero of each episode, they chose a look-alike and sound-alike for the remarkable character actor, Sir C. Aubrey Smith, as he portrayed a story-telling former British Army officer in 1939's British film, *The Four Feathers*.

In the 1:30 cartoon series, this tall, distinguished-looking, mustached, pipe-smoking story-teller would become Commander McBragg, sitting in his club and tale-spinning to a fellow member who would often try to escape but could not.

"There!" the Commander would say, punching a finger at the world globe beside him, "the burning desert of India. I was alone and without water. My camel's leg was broken, and suddenly in the distance, I could see a giant dust storm rushing toward me. What could I do?"

Whatever he did would always be something so utterly outlandish that it had to be appreciated by his fellow club member and the TV audience. The formula was perfect. All Buck and Chet had to do was come up

Actor Sir C. Aubrey Smith, the model and voice (imitated) for Commander McBragg.

with the impossible problem and the outlandish solution—the big lie - and the episode almost wrote itself.

The concept was roundly approved by Gordon Johnson and then by General Mills, and the first episodes of *The World of Commander McBragg* went into production in June of 1964.

ANOTHER ELEMENT

Having stock-piled an abundance of "Hunter" episodes, General Mills wanted another 4:30 inner element to fill out new series. This request resulted in ToTal TeleVision's icy offering, "Klondike Kat."

A bumbling Royal Mountie in the snow-covered Northwest, Klondike Kat is assigned to Fort Frazzle under the addle-brained command of Major Minor. For Klondike and his giant sled dog, Malamut, crime always seems to involve the villainous French mouse, Savoir Faire. And although Klondike constantly vows, "I'm gonna make mincemeat out of that mouse!", he never quite succeeds, perhaps because, as the French mouse is often heard to shout, "Savoir Faire is *everywhere!*"

Storylines & Summaries

THE WORLD OF COMMANDER McBRAGG
Storylines

#1	**Over the Falls**	How Commander McBragg went over the Ranchapokee Falls to escape a thousand savage savages.
#2	**Fish Story**	How Commander McBragg caught the world's biggest fish.
#3	**The Himalayas**	How Commander McBragg climbed the Himalayas and defeated the abominable snowmen.
#4	**The North Pole**	How Commander McBragg used the North Pole to outwit ferocious polar bears.
#5	**Khyber Pass**	How Commander McBragg escaped from the ambush by Ali By and his ten thousand screaming tribesmen at Khyber Pass.
#6	**The Ace of Aces**	How Commander McBragg as a flying ace brought down five enemy planes single-handed.
#7	**Niagara Falls**	How Commander McBragg went over Niagara Falls partly in a barrel.
#8	**Dodge City**	How Commander McBragg cleaned up Dodge City—the wildest town in the West.
#9	**Football by Hex**	How Commander McBragg won the game for his old Alma Mater—HEX.

#10   **Rabelasia**   How Commander McBragg set some kind of record by outwitting the entire Secret Service of Rabelasia.

#11   **Okeefenokee Swamp**   How Commander McBragg captured the world's largest black snake.

#12   **The Flying Machine**   How Commander McBragg invented the airplane without getting credit for it.

#13   **The Giant Elephant**   How Commander McBragg won the friendship of a giant elephant.

#14   **The Giant Bird**   How Commander McBragg was held captive by the giant bird.

#15   **Chicago Mobsters**   How Commander McBragg cleaned out the Chicago racketeers.

#16   **The Monster Bear**   How Commander McBragg was shipwrecked on the coldest islands in the world and defeated the Monster Bear.

#17   **The Kangaroo**   How Commander McBragg captured the world's strongest boxing Kangaroo.

#18   **The Giant Mosquito**   How Commander McBragg was attacked by a giant mosquito in the North Swamps.

#19   **The Black Knight**   How Commander McBragg encountered the Black Knight and won the day.

#20   **The Flying Pond**   How Commander McBragg was lost on the great Blue Mountain and caught a flock of ducks for dinner.

#21   **The Old Ninety-Two**   How Commander McBragg engineered the old Ninety-Two into Abilene on time with a load on—of fish.

#22   **Our Man in Manhattan**   How Commander McBragg delivered top secret papers to headquarters on the 50th floor of the Empire State Building—from the outside.

#23   **Oyster Island**   How Commander McBragg fought the giant oyster for the world's biggest pearl.

#24   **The Steam Car**   How Commander McBragg nearly invented the horseless carriage.

#25   **Swimming the Atlantic**   How Commander McBragg swam from England to the USA and ended up in the wrong ocean.

#26	**Fort Apache**	How Commander McBragg fought off the Indians at Fort Apache—just for the record.
#27	**The Flying Trapeze**	How Commander McBragg became the star of the flying trapeze.
#28	**Around the World**	How Commander McBragg was attacked by savages at Galungy Gorge, while ballooning around the world in 79 days.
#29	**Indianapolis Speedway**	How Commander McBragg won the Indianapolis 500-mile race with his own kind of jet racer.
#30	**The Rhino Charge**	How Commander McBragg's good deed for a cricket saved him from a charging rhino.
#31	**Mystifying McBragg**	How Commander McBragg, as "Mystifying McBragg, the Magician," was almost trapped in his famous underwater escape act.
#32	**Mammoth Caverns**	How Commander McBragg fired the world's most powerful gun and discovered the famous Mammoth Caverns.
#33	**The Astronaut**	How Commander McBragg orbited the earth for an all-time record thirty days.
#34	**The Flood**	How Commander McBragg saved River City from destruction by flood.
#35	**The Firing Squad**	How Commander McBragg escaped from a band of pygmies, while on a motion picture expedition of an eclipse on the Matusi Plains of Africa.
#36	**Ship of the Desert**	How Commander McBragg escaped a savage desert tribe thanks to his fast thinking with his camel.
#37	**Egypt**	How Commander McBragg, as an advance scout, wrecked his jeep against a pile of stones, and was hopelessly surrounded by the enemy, when the thought of one of Egypt's landmarks saved the day.

#38 The Singing Cowboy — How Commander McBragg, as the original singing cowboy, used his beautiful voice and handy guitar to escape a band of Apache Indians on the warpath.

#39 The Lumberjack — How Commander McBragg, in a daring feat of lumber work, almost got caught in a log jam and how miraculously he came out.

#40 The Rodeo Camp — How Commander McBragg became the all-time rodeo champion in a wild and wooly saga which ends in a "Grand" climax.

#41 Echo Canyon — How Commander McBragg, carrying gold for the Pony Express, was nearly done in by thieves at Echo Canyon, until he remembered where he was.

#42 Tightrope — How Commander McBragg walked a tightrope across the Victoria Falls – a tale that'll leave you spinning.

#43 Lake Tortuga — How Commander McBragg fought a giant turtle to save the starving villagers at Lake Tortuga—a sizzling escapade!

#44 Coney Island — How Commander McBragg was nearly left high and dry in trying to win the high-dive contest.

#45 Rainbow Island — How Commander McBragg flew a plane, took a picture and chased a rainbow all in his own special way.

#46 The Insect Collector — How Commander McBragg once bagged a lion in Africa without firing a shot—a story the commander magnifies out of even his usual proportion.

#47 Lost Valley — How Commander McBragg came to the aid of the Giant of the Lost Valley—a story with a twist.

#48 The Orient Express — How Commander McBragg outwitted the enemy Secret Service on the Orient Express—in his pajamas!

UNDERDOG
Later Story Summaries

STORYLINES FOR THE UNDERDOG SHOW

#53
Part One

"Pain Strikes Underdog"
Sweet Polly Purebred's plan to celebrate Underdog's birthday has to be put off when Underdog gets a call to guard the Excalibur Sword Collection on its way from one museum to another. On the way, sure enough, the crook, Riff Raff, and his gang hold up the train but Underdog saves the day, except that he's stricken with a terrible pain in his back and it looks like trouble ahead for Underdog.

#54
Part Two

"Pain Strikes Underdog"
At the hospital, Underdog explains that while he stays straight, he's right as rain, but when he bends over, there's a stabbing pain. Great doctors come from everywhere to examine Underdog, but in the meantime Riff Raff and his hoods steal the Excalibur Sword Collection, no longer guarded by Underdog, and Polly is worried because the next day will be Underdog's birthday.

#55
Part Three

"Pain Strikes Underdog"
Riff Raff and his gang have stolen the Excalibur Sword Collection while Underdog is in the hospital to find why there's a stabbing pain in his back every time he bends over. Now Riff Raff decides to hide the swords by covering them with wax as giant candles at a candle factory he takes over. Sweet Polly Purebred, in search of candles for Underdog's birthday cake, comes to the factory, is caught by Riff Raff's crooks, tied up and put on the assembly line to be made into a candle.

#56
Part Four

"Pain Strikes Underdog"
Underdog, from the hospital, hears Polly's cries for help from the candle factory where Riff Raff has tied her to the assembly line, and every moment she is taken nearer to the wick cutter. Although Underdog cannot bend without feeling a stabbing pain, he goes immediately to Polly's

rescue. When he attacks, he is tripped and falls on the assembly line where, because of his pain, he is unable to bend to get up. Riff and his hoods grab the candles hiding the stolen Excalibur swords and run. Underdog, however, finds a way to use the wick cutter to free himself and Polly and then capture Riff and the candles. Underdog melts the candles to find the swords – all but one, which turns out to be the cause of his stabbing pain, and a happy birthday is had by all.

#57
Part One

"The Molemen"

While Underdog is away on one of his missions, food crops begin disappearing all over the world. Sweet Polly Pure-bred, unable to contact Underdog, tries to get to the bottom of the mystery and falls into a deep cavern where she is made prisoner by Mange, King of the Molemen, who tells her that it is the Molemen who have been pulling all the crops underground to starve the earth people and then Mange will become ruler of all the earth. Polly is sure Underdog can stop Mange, but Mange shows Polly the Molehole gun which can make holes in anything - maybe even Underdog!

#58
Part Two

"The Molemen"

Underdog at last hears Sweet Polly Purebred's cries for help and comes to her rescue only to be confronted by the Molehole gun of Mange, King of the Molemen. Although the Molehole gun doesn't defeat Underdog it weakens him enough, already tired from his mission just completed, that the Giant Ant overcomes Underdog. He and Polly are both taken to the caterpillar cage to be sealed in a cocoon.

#59
Part Three

"The Molemen"

Just when Underdog and Sweet Polly Purebred are about to be sealed in a cocoon in the caterpillar cage of the Molemen, Underdog remembers his vitamin ring and takes one of his secret strength pills. Quickly, Underdog attacks the giant spider which has just captured Polly, but just as he defeats the spider, Polly falls again into the hands of Mange, King of the

Molemen, who threatens her with the Molehole gun if
Underdog doesn't do everything he (Mange) says.

#60   **"The Molemen"**
Part Four   Sweet Polly Purebred is threatened by the Molehole gun if
                Underdog does anything to stop Mange and the Molemen
                from conquering the earth. The people of earth have no
                food left—only water—and are too weak to fight these
                Molemen. But Underdog puts his secret energy vitamin
                pills in the water, after freeing Polly from her guard. Then
                he defeats Mange and his Molehole gun, and the earth is
                safe forever from the Molemen.

#61   **"The Flying Sorcerers"**
Part One   Underdog thinks he hears noises coming from a distant
                planet, and he is right. King Kup of the planet of the Flying
                Sorcerers is frantic for a baker to make good cakes. He
                sends his sons, Bric and Brac, to several other planets to try
                their bakers but no one will do. Then King Kup tunes in
                on Sweet Polly's earth TV show as she gives her recipe for
                chocolate cake, and King Kup immediately sends Bric and
                Brac to capture her.

#62   **"The Flying Sorcerers"**
Part Two   Bric and Brac, King Kup's sons from the Planet of the
                Flying Sorcerers, come to earth to capture Sweet Polly
                Purebred. Shoeshine is told by one of his customers that
                the ones who stopped to ask for directions to Polly's TV
                station are really Flying Sorcerers. Quickly Shoeshine
                becomes Underdog and chases Bric and Brac as they leave
                Earth with Polly. They battle terrifically and manage to fly
                so fast that they hide themselves and Polly from Underdog.
                Just when he catches up with them, Bric and Brac sorcer
                Underdog into a rubber ball.

#63   **"The Flying Sorcerer"**
Part Three Sweet Polly Purebred, captured by Bric and Brac, sons of
                King Kup of the planet of the Flying Sorcerers, is ordered
                to bake cake, and the King likes it so much that he orders

her to make fifty cakes, and then 500. Underdog, who has been sorced into a rubber ball, keeps breaking the Sorcerer's spell only to be put under the spell again. Polly, helpless, finally falls, exhausted, into the huge mixing bowl full of batter for the 500 cakes she is mixing.

#64
Part Four

"The Flying Sorcerers"
Underdog, bound into a rubber ball by the spell of the Flying Sorcerers, at last hears Polly cry for help as she sinks in the giant mixing bowl she was using to make cakes as the baking slave of King Kup. With the help of one of his energy vitamin pills he gains enough strength to break the spell for good and defeat all the flying Sorcerers and save Polly. King Kup promises never to do harm to anyone again and Polly gives him her cake recipe.

#65
Part One

"The Forget-Me-Net"
Simon Barsinister, mad scientist, determined to defeat Underdog, invents a "forget-me-net" which, when dropped over anyone's head, instantly makes him forget who and what he is. Simon tries it on the first victim who comes along and it works perfectly. Then he sets out to "net" Underdog.

#66
Part Two

"The Forget-Me-Net"
Simon Barsinister and his stooge, Cad Lackey, set out with the forget-me-net to "net" Underdog and instantly make him forget who he is. To attract Underdog, they commit various crimes but Underdog is always busy somewhere else. Finally Simon decides to "net" Sweet Polly Purebred as the only sure way to attract Underdog.

#67
Part Three

"The Forget-Me-Net"
Simon Barsinister and Cad attract Underdog to the forget-me-net by capturing first, Sweet Polly Purebred. They "net" Polly and she immediately forgets who she is. Underdog comes to the rescue and he, too, is "netted" and immediately forgets who he is. However, every time he hears his name, his memory comes back. Simon "nets" Underdog again and checks his "Fiendish Machinery" book. Learning

the trouble, Simon disguises Underdog as a little old lady apple peddler. Then Simon decides to make a forget-me-net big enough to cover the entire city of Washington.

#68 Part Four	**"The Forget-Me-Net"**

#68
Part Four

"The Forget-Me-Net"
While Simon makes a huge forget-me-net big enough to cover the city of Washington, Sweet Polly Purebred, who has been "netted" and has lost her memory meets, Apple Mary, the disguise Simon has put on Underdog, also a victim of the forget-me-net. "Apple Mary" goes through names with Polly until, saying her name, Polly's memory returns. Then Polly realizes that she is talking to Underdog, but that he has lost his memory. Just in time, Underdog is able to capture Simon and Cad in their own forget-me-net, as they approach Washington.

#69
Part One

"Guerrilla Warfare"
Underdog begins a new assignment guarding the priceless painting "Whistlers Father" at the museum's art show. Riff Raff calls his gang to get the painting by different tactics – guerrilla warfare.

#70
Part Two

"Guerrilla Warfare"
Riff Raff teaches his gang Guerrilla Warfare tactics to steal the painting Underdog is guarding. The gang tries out its "Hit & Run" attack, but fails. Riff announces his next tactic: camouflage and sabotage.

#71
Part Three

"Guerrilla Warfare"
Underdog has to think and work fast to keep Riff Raff and gang from stealing, by camouflage and sabotage, the painting Underdog guards. Desperate Riff next plans the sneak attack method!

#72
Part Four

"Guerrilla Warfare"
Riff Raff and gang, in a sneak attack, at last steal the painting Underdog is guarding. Underdog is almost revealed as Shoeshine until he thinks of a surprise to get back the painting and keep his secret.

#73   **"Simon Says – No Thanksgiving"**
Part One   Simon Barsinister, mad scientist, has a fiendish plan for
                 capturing the entire city thanks to two special buttons he's
                 installed across Main Street.

#74   **"Simon Says – No Thanksgiving"**
Part Two   Simon Barsinister is about to take over the city by pushing
                 two special buttons, but just as he begins to cross the street
                 to the buttons, the Thanksgiving Day Parade begins and
                 blocks his way. Simon immediately uses his "Time Bomb"
                 to go back in time and do away with Thanksgiving to stop
                 the parade.

#75   **"Simon Says – No Thanksgiving"**
Part Three   Underdog and Sweet Polly Purebred learn that Simon
                 Barsinister has gone back in time by using a "Time Bomb"
                 to do away with Thanksgiving. By using one of Simon's
                 bombs, they also join the Pilgrims and Indians just in time
                 to see what Simon plans to do.

#76   **"Simon Says – No Thanksgiving"**
Part Four   Simon Barsinister has tricked the Pilgrims and Indians into
                 fighting each other because Simon wants to get rid of
                 Thanksgiving. Underdog brings peace again just in time to
                 bring Thanksgiving back. As Simon begins crossing Main
                 Street to push his special buttons, suddenly the Thanksgiv-
                 ing Day Parade is on again, and Simon never gets across
                 the street…

GO GO GOPHERS
Selected Story Summaries

STORYLINES FOR *GO GO GOPHERS*

#14   **"He's For the Berries"**
            Colonel Kit Coyote tells his Sergeant to be sure to wake him after
            the Colonel takes a short nap because they're planning to go berry
            picking. The Colonel and Sarg go out to look for berries and
            Ruffled Feather and Running Board, knowing that the Colonel is
            near the patch of wild Gopher berries, fear for the consequences.

Despite the Sarg's warning, the Colonel eats some Gopher berries and immediately becomes a giant. He quickly decides that a giant is just what will scare off the two Gopher Indians. After several near misses, the giant Colonel traps the Indians but at that moment he shrinks down to midget size. As he begs for mercy, he is awakened by the Sergeant and it has all been a dream!

#15 **"Swamped"**
When the Colonel and Sarg plan to attack Ruffled Feather and Running Board from the rear through Soggy Swamp, the Sarg warns of alligators, but the Colonel is sure they've been cleared out long ago. The Indians build an "alligator submarine" and the fun begins. The Colonel and Sarg finally make it to the Indian tepee, only to meet with a final surprise.

#16 **"Tanks to Gophers"**
The Colonel receives his newest weapon in his constant fight with those two Indians, Ruffled Feather and Running Board. The Colonel tells the Sarg that it could take a catastrophe to stop an Army tank. The Indians go to work and, after a series of catastrophes, the Colonel is sure he has finally won but is sent flying, instead. The Colonel still calls for tanks, but the Sergeant only says, "You're welcome!"

#17 **"Indian Treasure"**
As the Colonel plots with Sarg to find a new way to catch the Gopher Indians, a stone lands in his office carrying with it a map of the "lost treasure of the Gopher Indians." The Colonel is immediately hot on the trail following the advice of a "tall, friendly Indian" who looks suspiciously to Sarg like Running Board and Ruffled Feather in disguise. From this point things for the Colonel only go from bad to worse.

#18 **"The Horseless Carriage Trade**
Ruffled Feather and Running Board, those two Gopher Indians, decide to buy a horse and wagon but instead, thanks to a fast-talking salesman, end up with a *horseless* carriage. After a wild ride, they decide they've had enough and should trade it to the Colonel for his horse and wagon. The Colonel

tells the Sarg that this is the chance to drive away those Indians. He challenges them to race—if the Indians win they can trade for his horse and wagon—if The Colonel and Sarg win, the Indians will have to leave Gopher Gulch. Guess who gets to stay in Gopher Gulch!

#19   **"Honey Fun"**
The Colonel finds while checking Army supplies with the Sarg that jars of honey are missing. Colonel Coyote immediately suspects the Gopher Indians, Ruffled Feather and Running Board. He's right, of course, and one Gopher Trick after another finally leads him straight to the bear facts.

#20   **"The Colonel Cleans Up"**
The Colonel has a new secret weapon—a giant vacuum cleaner—which he's sure will clean up things in Gopher Gulch, meaning those two Gopher Indians, Ruffled Feather and Running Board. However, no matter what the Sarg and Colonel do with the cleaner, the Indians pull the switch on them!

#21   **"The Raw Recruits"**
        (Part One of the "Indians in the Army")
Colonel Kit Coyote tells Sarg that if they can't make the last two Gopher Indians in Gopher Gulch leave, The Colonel will draft them into the Army. As new "recruits" Ruffled Feather and Running Board are introduced to drilling and the obstacle course, but you-know-who gets drilled and runs into most of the obstacles.

#22   **"Tenshun"**
        (Part Two of the "Indians in the Army")
The Colonel, still determined to make soldiers out of those two Gopher Indians, Ruffled Feather and Running Board, takes them from the rifle range. which they've left in shambles. and decides to show them how to march. This also ends in disaster. Next the Colonel and Sarg show the Indians how to shoot the cannons, and the Colonel really ends up in the air over this mess!

#23   **"Cuckoo Combat"**
(Part Three of the" Indians in the Army")
The Colonel, having failed to teach those two Gopher Indians, Ruffled Feather and Running Board, any other phase of Army life, now demonstrates to them man-to-man combat tactics. The Colonel throws himself enthusiastically into this training, but he's the one, of course, who gets thrown!

#24   **"Kitchen Capers"**
(Part Four of the "Indians in the Army")
The Colonel has drafted those two Gopher Indians, Ruffled Feather and Running Board, into the Army and they have ruined the rifle range, obstacle course and drill field. The Colonel decides kitchen duty is the only answer. This really gets the Colonel into the soup until he gets blown out by gunpowder biscuits.

#25   **"The Great White Stallion"**
Colonel Kit Coyote is convinced that only with the fastest horse in the territory will he ever catch those two Gopher Indians, Ruffled Feather and Running Board. The Sergeant says that would be "The Great White Stallion" a famous wild horse. The Gophers get word that The Colonel is hunting the Great White Stallion and climb promptly into their two-man horse costume, and the horsing around begins!

#26   **"Blankety Blank Blanket"**
Those two Gopher Indians, Ruffled Feather and Running Board, chilled by the winter winds of Gopher Gulch, hold up a stagecoach and take from one of the lady passengers a nice, big, warm blanket. The Colonel and Sarg are hot on the Indians' trail, with the Colonel vowing to the lady passenger that he'll get the blanket for her. How the Colonel keeps his promise spins quite a yarn.

#27   **"The Unsinkable Ironclad"**
Colonel Kit Coyote orders another secret weapon in his long fight against those two Gopher Indians, Running Board and Ruffled Feather. This time the Colonel tells his Sarg that the unsinkable Ironclad battleship will do the trick. The Gophers get

the signal, and in the end the "unsinkable" Ironclad isn't the only thing that gets taken down the river.

#28   **"Amusement Park"**
The Colonel, tired of chasing those two Gopher Indians, Ruffled Feather and Running Board, invites the Sarg to forget differences in rank and go with him for fun at the amusement park. No sooner do they arrive, than the manager tells them the Gophers are insisting the park is on their land and are taking free rides all over the park. The chase is on and it's a carnival of errors!

#29   **"Losing Weight" (Or "Crash Diet")**
Those two Gopher Indians, Ruffled Feather and Running Board, send the Colonel a phony message from General Nuisance stating that if he is still overweight in one week's time, Colonel Coyote will be discharged from the Army. Then the Indians tell the Colonel they've heard he wants to lose weight and they can help with an old Indian weight losing plan. The Colonel is eager and the Indians put him through the works as they gorge themselves on the Army's supplies. When the Colonel is a complete shambles, General Nuisance arrives unexpectedly and the Colonel learns the unexpected truth!

TENNESSEE TUXEDO
Sample Story Summaries

STORYLINES FOR *TENNESSEE TUXEDO*
#53   **"Smilin' Yak's Service – Flying & Aviation"**
Yak inherits an airplane but doesn't know what to do with it, until Tennessee Tuxedo decides that they will go into the airplane business. After a breathtaking flight, in which Tennessee proves to Yak and Chumley that he can't fly a plane, they decide they're not ready for business, but Rocky Monanoff, the crook, orders them to be ready to take him for a fast ride after his "bank business." Tennessee and friends hurry to Mr. Whoopee, man with all the answers, and learn enough about planes to have one more wild ride before Officer Badge catches Rocky Monanoff, thanks to Tennessee's unskilled piloting.

#54   **"Teddy Bear Trouble – Finger Painting"**

No sooner has a Koala Bear from Australia joined Stanley Livingston's zoo than he disappears, and Stanley finds him with Tennessee Tuxedo and Chumley. Stanley threatens to make Tennessee leave the zoo if the Teddy Bear gets out of his own cage again. But night after night a mysterious visitor lets the bear out and he greets Tennessee the next morning at Tennessee's house. Tennessee and Chumley ask Mr. Whoopee, man with all the answers, for help and he tells them all about tracking down suspects with fingerprinting. None of the fingerprints they collect from other zoo inmates match the prints on the bear's cage door, but by staying up all night, Tennessee catches Chumley letting the bear out. Then Tennessee knows just what's wrong – Chumley has missed his old toy teddy bear which has been lost in a closet.

#55   **"Sword Play – How Steel Is Made"**

Tennessee Tuxedo doesn't like the job Stanley Livingston, keeper of the zoo, gives him—cleaner of the museum. As Tennessee sweeps, he notices a suit of armor and Tennessee pretends he's a knight in battle. He swings the broom and accidentally hits the suit of armor. The metal head piece falls on Tennessee and knocks him out. While "out" he imagines that King Stanley sends Knight Sir Tennessee out to fight the fire-eating dragon. Tennessee and Chumley keep losing the battles to the dragon until they go to Mr. Whoopee, man with all the answers, who tells them all about how steel is made and how Damascus became famous for its fine steel swords. Even with a steel sword, the dragon tricks Tennessee, who "comes to" just in time to be in real trouble with Stanley.

#56   **"Funny Money – Printing"**

Tennessee Tuxedo, Chumley and Baldy start a printing company. Their first customer, Rocky Monanoff, the crook, wants ten thousand pictures of George Washington printed in green and leaves a sample for them to copy from. Tennessee and friends soon discover they don't know how to work the machinery and go to Mr. Whoopee, man with all the answers. He tells them about different types of printing presses, and just as they are leaving, Whoopee discovers the "job" Monanoff has told them to do. Thanks to the tip off, Officer Badge gets there just in time...

KING LEONARDO AND HIS SHORT SUBJECTS
**The Original Story Summaries
and Storylines Used
to Sell the Series**

**King Leonardo And His Short Subjects
"The King And Odie" – First 26 Episodes**

1.   **"Riches To Rags"**
        Itchy and Biggy capture Odie. Itchy tells King he has reformed,
        says King must go among people because he has lost touch.
        While King is gone, Itchy and Biggy take over, masquerading as
        King and Odie. Odie gets free to unmask the evil twosome.

2.   **"Drumming Up The Bongos"**
        All the orders for Bongo Drums stop coming in. Biggy and Itchy
        are stealing them. Economy starts to collapse. Odie and King
        think USA has stopped ordering drums, must go and find out
        why. Biggy and Itchy sabotage trip. Odie, at last minute, gets
        hold of drum orders to save King from being unseated.

3.   **"Synthetic Smell"**
        Itchy and Biggy get Professor Messer to devise "smell" formula
        which they make up and spread about the kingdom. People
        blame Odie Colognie, and insist he be thrown out of Kingdom.
        To King, it looks like it's either no throne or no Odie, but,
        Odie—before the complaining subjects—catches Biggy and
        Itchy with the Big Smell.

4.   **"War On The Congo"**
        Biggy and Itchy convince rival country—Koko Loco—that
        King Leonardo intends to make war to get all of Bongo drum
        business. Koko Loco prepares to attack and word reaches Bongo
        Congo by way of the Bongo drummers. Odie has idea: uses
        surprise "Bongo attack" on enemy troops, all of King
        Leonardo's subjects playing a hot Conga. Enemy troops are
        unable to resist—drop their guns and join the Conga dancing
        chain.

5.   **"Duel To The Dearth"**
Biggy and Itchy convince people that King is coward, insist on duel to prove bravery worthy of a king. Biggy imports Killer Kannon for cannon duel, sword duel, spear duel, etc. Although Odie always manages to make King win, Biggy keeps saying not enough…until Odie comes up with "fool-proof" way to show King's bravery.

6.   **"Bringing Up Biggy"**
Leonardo tells Odie story of how his own brother—Itchy—ever got tied up with a crook like Biggy Rat. We see Itchy and Biggy as boys along with Biggy's father, Big Daddy Rat. Father helps plan very first plot for Itchy to steal Leonardo's birthright. In telling story, King reminds Odie that it was he—Odie—in his first royal appearance who ruined this long ago plan.

7.   **"Paris Pursuit"**
King and Odie take vacation—springtime in Paris. Biggy and Itchy decide this ideal time to get rid of pair. Follow to Paris—aboard liner (plots foiled), aboard plane (plots again foiled). Finally, in Paris, the evil pair manage to get King and Odie tossed in prison. Only Odie's Bongo drum playing can save the day.

8.   **"Beatnik Boom"**
Biggy gets Itchy to start everyone being beatnik—no work, just sipping coffee and listening to poetry with Bongo background. Economy begins to collapse. Odie finally composes special Bongo song (rhythm), which makes everyone—even Itchy—want to work.

9.   **"Broken Boys"**
Leonardo and Odie talk about their boyhood—days when Odie's father was royal perfumer; how bosom buddies Odie and King were almost separated by plot of Itchy Brother and "Little Big" Rat—making Leonardo believe Odie had turned against him, ordering Odie dramatically out of castle. Only Odie's unswerving loyalty saves day.

10. **"Royal Amnesia"**

Accident to King (while he is alone) simultaneously ruins his mane and wipes out his memory. He wanders about—into all kinds of mischief—trying to find out who he is. Odie, back at palace, has to cover up as Biggy and Itchy get wind of King's disappearance. Odie makes dummies, tries to impersonate King, etc. Lucky blow—from Biggy—saves day by bringing back King's memory at moment Odie is about to be "done in."

11. **"Battleslip"**

Biggy and Itchy buy huge battleship and anchor off coast of Bongo Congo, start shelling palace and rest of kingdom. Every attempt by Odie and King to sink or capture ship fails since Bongo Congo has no Navy or Marines—only an army. Everything seems black until Odie gets gem of maneuver—drain out the water and reach the ship by land.

12. **"Super Sabotage"**

Bridges fall, trains collide, planes fall as Biggy and Itchy embark on stepped up campaign of sabotage. Then: "Workers arise—friends of Itchy, too" is the call heard down at the Bongo drum factory. "Share the wealth; down with the King." People storm the palace, blaming the King for hoarding wealth and failing to properly build roads, railroads, etc. As King Leonardo waits bravely for the final blow, Odie proves sabotage of Biggy and Itchy is to blame for problems.

13. **"The Big Freeze"**

Biggy decides the only way to get rid of Leonardo and put Itchy on the throne is to bump the King off. Itchy and Biggy get mass of assassination weapons—new and old—but Odie manages to turn each attempt around so that it backfires on the devilish duo…until the last weapon—the freeze ray—is used on King. Situation seems static and frozen until Odie brilliantly thinks of "getting King into hot water." King melts—all is saved.

14.   *"Perfume Panic"*
Suddenly, all perfume made in Bongo Congo has terrible smell.
Biggy and Itchy are ruining entire supply—even though it is
made right inside palace. Odie Colognie—keeper of Poppa
Colognie's secret formula for perfume—is blamed and at-
tacked—by the women, by the men, almost by the King. Odie
goes undercover to find what Biggy and Itchy are doing, but has
no success. His sister, Nosie Colognie, sticks her nose into his
business and saves his neck—starts fad for the horrible perfume:
"It's the latest thing, and everyone's wearing one of the new stylish
gold clothespins on the nose."

15.   *"Sticky Stuff"*
Without apparent reason, King begins sticking to everything he
touches. Odie always manages to free him, although a little
roughly at times. We see Biggy and Itchy in lab with Professor
Messer trying to perfect permanent glue formula. Finally do—
after some explosive times in the lab. Biggy and Itchy put final
formula on King's bed, then dramatically announce that King is
done. To prove them wrong, King must appear. If not, Itchy will
rightfully take the throne. The subjects agree, and all looks lost.
But Odie comes through again: Saws off enough of bed so that a
stiff Leonardo can put in an appearance.

16.   *"Lyin' Lion"*
Professor Messer invents for Biggy and Itchy mechanical Leonardo
and Odie which Biggy and Itchy can control by just *their* voices.
All they need say is, "Get 'em boys," and the monsters attack
anyone. People think their royalty has gone crazy. Finally, Biggy
and Itchy bring mechanical monsters to palace to "take over" but,
in nick of time, Odie lights up: Puts his talents to use by imitating
Biggy's voice perfectly. Contradictory orders—from the real and
unreal Biggy—so confuse mechanical monsters that they explode.

17.   **"Goldcrush"**
Biggy and Itchy discover gold mine under palace. They devise
diabolical methods for getting King to move palace and sell land:
the moat overflows, washing King out to sea; mosquitoes are

imported; etc. King is ready to sell, but Odie smells a Rat. Still, he has no proof and must follow King's orders. Goes down to basement to pack royal heirlooms, and sees fresh dirt, discovers mine and saves gold for the kingdom.

18. **"No Bong Bongo"**
Sabotage again as Biggy and Itchy get jobs in Bongo factory (against Itchy's will). They make skins too skinny, and the bong goes out of the Bongos. USA will have to give business to Koko Loco; economy starts to collapse. Odie saves the day: Soaks drums, and skins get tight, so there's once more bong in the Bongo—and, Odie exposes Biggy and Itchy dressed in factory clothes.

19. **"Storm The Palace"**
Biggy and Itchy get weather-making machines from Professor Messer and put to use in kingdom. Monsoons, snow out of season, etc. Then they turn on the dry spell and all of the growing food withers away. Subjects blame the King (as Biggy eggs them on), claiming bad weather caused by secret royal experiments. Looks like rebellion until Odie calls in brother—Stinky Colognie—to make things right: "Even the sun runs from Stinky." And the kingdom goes wet, and happily back to normal.

20. **"Gallopin' Gambles"**
Biggy and Itchy are taking over by way of the underworld game. Biggy has imported hoodlums, and they are corrupting the kingdom. People are gambling on anything. There are dog races and hog races; cat races and rat races, hare races and mare races. All the kingdom's earnings are going into Biggy's gambling syndicate. The country is falling apart. Families are starving. King outlaws gambling, but to no avail. Finally, Odie steps in. Talks to all the dogs and hogs and cats and rats and hares and mares—gets them to fix a race so that people win. Biggy and Itchy are broken.

21. **"De-Based Ball"**
It's the Bongo Bruins versus the Koko Kards getting ready for their series games. All of Bongo Congo is waiting. They have long been dissatisfied because they haven't won a series in 432

years. King and Odie are confident because King is pitching, Odie is catching—but practice session just before game shows everything going wrong. Biggy has gotten special "jumping ball" from Professor Messer, and Itchy—in disguise—is umpire. Looks hopeless until Odie get his Uncle, Sintilatin Skunk, to come up with jumping bat.

22. **"Air Sick"**
Biggy and Itchy buy huge bomber and star to work on palace and kingdom. King and Odie build special anti-aircraft weapons (sling-shots firing Bongo drums, etc.), but are unable to bring down plane. Biggy and Itchy dropping every conceivable type of bomb—gas bomb, bug bomb, bon bomb, etc. Palace being destroyed. Things looks black until Odie thinks of Rock Raven, an old guided missile friend. The plane topples.

23. **"Imported Imposter"**
Itchy tells Biggy about Long Lost Louie Lion who would rightfully be king now if he hadn't vanished years ago. Biggy gets picture of Louie and has Itchy help him get stand-in from Koko Loco. Leonardo and Odie, broken as "Louie" triumphantly returns, bow out, but Odie gets rumor that Louie may be imposter. Meantime, Louie has turned on Biggy and Itchy—taking over for himself after belting them around (he is huge). Finally, Odie learns true identity of imposter and dramatically lets Leonardo strip Lost Louie of his costume and power—Louie is actually a tiny kitten in disguise.

24. **"Counterfeit Colognie"**
Odie is kidnapped and held for ransom—tremendous amount of money which King has difficult time raising. He pays. However, when Odie returns to palace, he is really Biggy in disguise. Biggy works to foul King completely—physically and otherwise—until King's regime is in disrepute. Then, Biggy calls for Itchy to leave Odie and come to take throne. Looks bad, but when Itchy arrives and takes over, he is really Odie in disguise.

25.   **"Fatal Fever"**

By way of few hidden blows on head and a few fixed palace subjects who say what they are told to say, Biggy and Itchy convince King he is ill—suffering from the famous Fatal Fever. Pretending to be doctor, Biggy sends King to sanitarium. Odie goes along, and Biggy and Itchy put into action their plans for bumping off the twosome. All fail, until "Vise Room." where walls start coming together to crush our heroes. Hope seems gone until he remembers that the royal mane of Leonardo is stronger than anything in the world. Walls are stopped. When Biggy and Itchy come to drag their victims away, they are captured.

26.   **"Dim Gem"**

The King and Odie head for London on a most important mission: The royal jewels are dirty and must be polished by the best polisher in the world. According to a special paper the King read (planted by Biggy) the best jeweler is in London, and his name is Scratchy Jewel (who turns out to be Itchy in disguise). The jewels are stolen and Odie turns to Spotland Guard. But it is really Odie who gets back jewels by opening a Beatnik coffee shop in the heart of London. Itchy, wearing half the jewels, falls into trap—and then leads them to Biggy, who has the rest of the jewels.

King Leonardo and His Short Subjects
The Hunter – First 26 Episodes

1.   **"The Brookloined Bridge"**

Fox steals the Brooklyn Bridge. Traffic comes to a standstill; the city panics.Only one man for the job—The Hunter.

2.   **"Counterfeit Wants"**

The Fox counterfeits wanted posters, selling them to people who want to "get rid" of someone—mayors, congressmen, relative, etc. For personal reasons, Fox also makes up millions of counterfeit posters of The Hunter—"Wanted Dead or Alive...suggest immediate hanging without trial."

3.   **"Haunted Hunter"**
     The Fox haunts City Hall. All officials leave. Mayor—from
     drugstore on the corner—calls in The Hunter. He—after much
     Ghostly action—finds mysterious holes in City Hall cellar.
     Eventually turns out Fox has buried treasure map and loot is
     under City Hall.

4.   **"Fort Knox Fox"**
     All of Fort Knox is lifted. Hunter locates Fox selling gold bricks
     for building homes with a sound foundation.

5.   **"Stealing A March"**
     All the sheet music for marches is stolen. Entire armies unable to
     move for lack of marching music. Special session of Congress
     called. The Hunter locates The Fox, but is told he will never
     know the hiding place of music unless Fox gets his freedom and
     huge ransom.

6.   **"Horn A-Plenty"**
     Embarrassment for The Hunter. His famous horn is stolen right
     from under his ear. He is unable to hunt. Finally borrows horn
     form his RCA Victor cousin, but is far from satisfactory. Locates
     Fox in Hollywood where he has sold horn at fabulous price for
     remake of Jack Bunny movie: Horn Blows Up at Midnight. The
     Hunter gets horn after explosion.

7.   **"Garbage Grabber"**
     Garbage everywhere is being stolen. Garbage collection compa-
     nies go broke. Union calls in The Hunter. He finds The Fox—
     having bought up garbage disposal trucks at cheap price—
     working extensive "Good Humor" racket with trucks that mix ice
     cream on the spot for extra freshness.

8.   **"The Underwear Scandal"**
     Everyone's underwear—including The Hunter's—is stolen.
     Hunter finds The Fox in Alaska selling the underwear at extra
     high prices.

9.   **"Lost Liner"**
Entire ship is stolen at sea. The Hunter locates The Fox in Central park selling rides on rather elaborate sight-seeing boat on lake.

10.   **"Risky Ransom"**
The Fox kidnaps The Hunter's nephew, Horrors Hunter. The kid, while Fox holds him for ransom, drives Fox nearly crazy.

11.   **"Not There Niagra"**
Suddenly, all reservoirs are freezing solid, Fox having sneaked in underground deep-freeze units. The Hunter ties this in with stolen Niagara Falls—finds the Fox selling "hot" water at high prices.

12.   **"Bombs Away"**
Top secret "D" bomb formula is stolen. Bomb makes anyone carrying it disappear completely. Fox opens "Disappearance Incorporated." The Hunter stumbles into capturing Fox just as Hunter, himself, as he prepares to blow his horn disappears.

13.   **"Armored Car Coup"**
Armored cars disappearing by hundreds. Hunter locates Fox selling 'homes' in Cold Crushia Land—homes perfect for keeping out cold, keeping sunlight off rugs and, when Secret Police come, just lock door from inside.

14.   **"Telephone Pole Wire"**
The Hunter gets a wire telling him telephone poles everywhere are being stolen. The Hunter locates Fox in new big business—selling pre-fab log cabins at low prices.

15.   **"Beau Peep's Sheep"**
Beau, on his way to give girlfriend present of flock, has all of his sheep stolen. Appeals to The Hunter, who locates Fox selling sure-fire method for getting to sleep.

16.   **"Rustler Hustler"**
        Entire herds of cattle are disappearing. The Hunter goes West on
        horseback, locates The Fox operating fake "Canyon" truck which
        cattle always run into.

17.   **"The Green Cheese Mystery"**
        Delicatessen owners everywhere going absolutely mad. Custom-
        ers ordering ham and cheese on rye, but there is no cheese—no
        cheese at all. The Hunter is called in and locates Fox—selling
        "small piece" of real estate on the moon.

18.   **"Great Train Robbery"**
        Painsalvania Freight train is stolen. The Hunter investigates.
        Thinks he has found train, but finds it is only millionaire's (Fox's)
        toy full-sized train which he has set up in backyard. Ransom note
        asks millions for return of refrigerated pum-plums which kids all
        over country are screaming for.

19.   **"Florida Fraud"**
        The Hunter is vacationing in Florida when an invasion from
        Mars is broadcast—by Fox, of course. Everyone rushes out of
        Florida. Fox saws off state and moves it out onto ocean. The
        Hunter locates him off coast of Britain, where Fox is selling
        tickets to giant amusement park.

20.   **"Planes Pfft"**
        The Hunter is called in when a number of passenger liners are
        stolen. Hunter stumbles onto secret when he goes on duck
        hunting trip where results are guaranteed. Fox, in disguise, is
        running "Duck Guide" racket with slogan: "Why wait in a cold
        duck blind. We bring you to the ducks."

21.   **"Race Horse Robbery"**
        Fastest horse in world is stolen just before big race. Hunter is
        called in. He ties in theft with masked bank bandit on horseback
        so fast police cars can't catch him. In mad chase after the Fox on
        the stolen horse, they get on race track and stolen horse wins
        race—Hunter on ice wagon animal—comes in second.

22. **"Purloined Parrots"**
    The Hunter is called in to investigate theft of parrots everywhere. Then, parrots are suddenly all being returned. The Hunter ties this mystery in with rapid rise in sales for Gookie Soda crackers, of which Fox—in disguise—is President. All of the returned parrots continually say, "Polly wants a gookie."

23. **"Girl Friday Fox"**
    The Hunter decides he should have Girl Friday like other private eyes. Runs ad and hires Friday Fox. Suddenly, much to Hunter's dismay, he begins to have many accidents. Further, his files are stolen, his furniture is stolen and even his clients are stolen. Hunter get suspicious of Friday Fox when he narrows down list of possible suspects.

24. **"Stamp Stick-Up"**
    Stamp collections are stolen across the country. The Hunter is called in. Finds Fox operating rival post office selling "speedy stamps"—already postmarked.

25. **"Statue of Liberty Play"**
    Mystery of the century. Government calls in The Hunter to locate the great statue. Hunter finally locates in Cold Crushia Land where Fox has been selling tickets to Crushians so they can see what Liberty looks like.

26. **"Private Eye Problem"**
    Rival business is opened up and The Hunter is losing all his customers. New "eye," Finder Fox, bears strange resemblance to The Fox; also, is amazingly able to solve any crime—almost as if he had planned the crime as well as its solution. After many cases, Hunter gets suspicious that there may be a "Tie-in" between this rival "eye" and the crimes, themselves.

King Leonardo and His Short Subjects
Toonerville Turtle – First 26 Episodes

1.   Two Gun Turtle (Fast On the Flaw)
2.   Stunted Pilot (Plane Failure)
3.   Sea Haunt (Follow The Fish)
4.   Highway Petrol (Road Blockhead)
5.   Knight of The Square Table (Suit of Harmer)
6.   Mish-Mash-Mush (Panting For Gold)
7.   The Unteachables (The Lawless Fears)
8.   King of Swat (Babe Rube)
9.   One Trillion B.C. (Dinosaur Dope)
10. Olimping Champion (Cripple Threat Athlete)
11. Stuporman (High Frying)
12. Buffaloed Bill (Custard's Last Stand)
13. Lossie (Doggone Dope)
14. Moon Goon (Spacehead)
15. Robin Hoodwink (Thimple Thief)
16. Shiverboat (Captains Outrageous)
17. Souse Painter (Brush Boob)
18. T-Turtle (Counterfeit Feat)
19. Railroad End-gineer (Crazy Jones)
20. Quarterback Hack (Pigskinned)
21. Over Where (Draft Head)
22. Lumberquack (Topped)
23. Bee Sweet (Buzz, Buzz, Buzz)
24. Jerky Jockey (Kenducky Derby)
25. Fired Fireman (Hook and Batter)
26. Paradrooper (Jump Jerk Jump)

We wish to thank the millions of fans who have made TTV characters, especially Underdog, so popular over the years. We hope this book will, at least in some small measure, show our appreciation.

Buck and Chet

Index

Adams, Don, 97-99, 100, 102,
        107, 110, 112-113,
        116, 125-125
Allen, Steve, 97-98, 119
Atlas, Charles, 109, 140
Baldy, 106, 177
Barney Fife, 109
Barrymore, Lionel, 133
Batman, 79, 82, 85
Biggy Rat, 54, 178-184
Bluto, 94
Cad Lackey, 2, 133, 157-159,
        170
Candid Camera, 119
Capp, Al, 66
Capp, Jerry, 66
Captain Marvel, 79, 82
Captain Nice, 155
Car 54, Where Are You?, 119
Carson, Johnny, 120
Cheerios Kid, 40
Chester Goode, 93

Chumley, 104, 114, 176-177
Clooney, Rosemary, 98
Colonel Kit Coyote, 100, 172-
        176
Colman, Ronald, 54
Commander McBragg, 160-166
Como, Perry, 97-98
Conried, Hans, 138
Courageous Cat, 84-86
Covington, Treadwell, 62-63, 65,
        67-69, 72
Cox, Wally, 116, 119-120, 122,
        125-128, 137
Crusader Rabbit, 54
Delmar, Kenny, 55, 73, 106
Discovery, 92
Doc Adams, 93
Dr. Gillespie, 132
Dr. Kildare, 132
Exploring, 92
Feldman, Eli, 62, 90
Fillmore, 138

Fonda, Henry, 116

Flunky, 106

Fox, The, 55, 63, 139, 184-188

Gamma Productions, 37-39, 43, 90

Go Go Gophers, 100, 180

Gomer Pyle, 79

Goulding, Ray, 6, 9, 80-81

Griffith, Andy, 79, 109

Gunsmoke, 90, 93

Hanks, Tom, 1-2

Hanna-Barbera, 48, 54

Heckle & Jeckle, 76

Hector Heathcote, 145

Henry (H.R.) Potter, 132

Hippity Hopper, 147

Hiram Holliday, 147

Honeymooners, The, 90

Hoppity Hooper, 138, 140, 147-148

Huckleberry Hound, 46, 55

Hunter, The, 22, 27, 102, 123, 161, 184-188

I Love Lucy, 18-29, 79-80, 84, 90

Ishi, Chris, 72

Itchy Brother, 54, 64, 73, 75

It's a Wonderful Life, 132

Johnson, Gordon, 5, 11-15, 27, 31, 35, 37-41, 43-44, 46, 49, 57-65, 67-69, 71-74, 76-78, 80, 86, 89, 91, 93, 110-113, 129, 134, 137-140, 143-144, 147, 161

Kane, Bob, 85

King Leonardo, 34, 53-54, 56, 61, 63-65, 73-76, 83, 178-184

Klondike Kat, 162

Knotts, Don, 109

Leonardo daVinci, 49, 53

Lewis N. Clark, 151-154

Loy, Myrna, 98

Major Minor, 162

Malamut, 162

Marshall, Mort, 106

Matt Dillon, 93

Matthes, Jack, 66-67

Menino, Thomas (Mayor), 2-3

Mighty Mouse, 91-92

Mr. Know-It-All, 38, 160

Mr. Peppers, 119

Mr. Terrific, 155

Mr. Wizard, 56, 63-64

Molly (Barker) Clark, 151-154

Monroe, Marilyn, 131, 137

Moore, Gary, 119

Morgan, Frank, 102

Odie Colognie, 54, 63-64, 75, 178-184

Pallette, Eugene, 53

Pangborn, Franklin, 106

Parrot Playhouse, 90, 93, 96, 110-111, 113

PAT (Leonardo), 74

Pelican Films, 62, 90, 110-111

Phinias J. Whoopee, 104-106, 176-177

Pieche, Peter, 74

Plattes, Cy, 13, 69, 92, 112, 138

Popeye, 94

Powell, William, 98

Purbeck, Nancy, 2

Raft, George, 133

Reading Room, 92

Reeves, George, 18, 32

Riff Raff, 3, 133-134, 157-159, 167-168, 171

Robinson, Edward G., 54

Rocky and Bullwinkle, 14, 36-38, 43, 48, 54, 160

Rocky Monanoff, 104-105, 176-177

Roosevelt, Teddy, 100

Rosenblum, "Slapsie," 54

Ruff and Reddy, 48, 54

Ruffled Feather, 100, 172-176

Running Board, 100, 172-176

Savoir Faire, 162

School House, 119

Senator Claghorn, 55, 73

Sergeant Badge, 105-106, 176-177

Sergeant, The, 100, 172-176

Sesame Street, 145

77 Sunset Strip, 120

Shoeshine Boy, 134, 138, 154, 159

Simon Barsinister, 2-3, 132-133, 157-159, 170-172

Smith, Sir C. Aubrey, 161

Sparks, Ned, 106

Spencer's Mountain, 116, 120

Spoofs and Saddles, 93, 95

Stanley Livingston, 106, 177

State Fair, 120

Sullivan, Ed, 98

Superman, 18-20, 80, 82, 130-131

Sweet Polly Purebread, 2-3, 131, 134, 156-157, 167-172

Swift, Allen, 73

Tennessee Tuxedo, 13, 27, 34, 87, 89, 103-105, 110-114, 176-177

Terry, Paul, 63

Terrytoons, 83

This Is Your Life, 90

Tooter Turtle, 56, 63, 189

Total TeleVision Productions (TTV), 57-60, 89-91, 140, 144-145, 147

Twinkles, 66-67, 69, 160

Underdog, 1-3, 5, 17, 26, 128-134, 136-141, 143-144, 147-149, 151, 153-161, 167-172

Upson, Stuart, 95

Victory Over Violence, Dedication

Waldo, 138

Waltons, The, 116

Ward and Scott, 14-15, 27, 34, 37-38, 40, 54, 71, 77, 85, 128, 147

Wayne, John, 100-101

Wizard of Oz, The, 102

Yak, 106

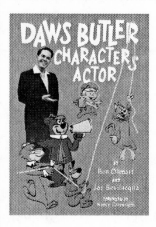